DRAWING
AND
PAINTING
FROM
NATURE

CATHY JOHNSON

DRAWING
AND
PAINTING
FROM
NATURE

CATHY JOHNSON

Design Press

CHAPTER-OPENER ILLUSTRATIONS

Figure 1-1 (page 9). *Dry River Maple,* razor-pointed felt-tipped pen, by Cathy Johnson. Figure 2-1 (page 21). *Tallgrass Prairie Habitat,* pen-and-ink, by Cathy Johnson. Reproduced courtesy of the Martha Lafite Thompson Nature Sanctuary, Liberty, Missouri. Figure 3-1 (page 36). *Bandits,* dry-brush watercolor applied over a wet-on-wet base, by Cathy Johnson. Figure 4-1 (page 50). *Rosemary,* crow-quill pen (part of a series illustrating an article on herbs), by Cathy Johnson. Reproduced courtesy of *Early American Life.* Figure 5-1 (page 62). *Family,* razor-pointed felt-tipped pen, by Cathy Johnson. Figure 6-1 (page 72). *Spring Falls,* china marker and pen on coquille board, by Cathy Johnson. Figure 7-1 (page 79). *Mineral Water Well,* pen-and-ink, by Cathy Johnson. Reproduced courtesy of the Excelsior Springs Department of Parks and Recreation. Figure 8-1 (page 93). *Great Horned Owl,* pen-and-ink sepia drawing, by Cathy Johnson. Figure 9-1 (page 105). This field sketchbook drawing proves—to me at least—that I really did see this teapot-handled tree! Figure 10-1 (page 112). Pencil drawing, by Cathy Johnson. Figure 11-1 (page 119). *Fox Squirrel,* ink on scratchboard, by Cathy Johnson. Reproduced courtesy of *Missouri Life Magazine.* Figure 12-1 (page 126). This piece beautifully exemplifies the printmaker's art. *Ringneck Duck,* by Ernest Lussier; print by Ann Lussier. Reproduced courtesy of the artist. Figure 13-1 (page 131). This drawing became a contemplative exercise as I lost myself in depicting the intricacies of the leaf and gall. Figure 14-1 (page 143). *Yellow Dock,* pen-and-ink, by Cathy Johnson.

First Edition, First Printing

Copyright © 1989 by Cathy Johnson
Printed in the United States of America
Designed by Gilda Hannah

Library of Congress Cataloging-in-Publication Data
Johnson, Cathy (Cathy A.)
  Drawing and painting from nature.

  Bibiliography: p.
  Includes index.
  1. Plants in art. 2. Animals in art. 3. Nature
(Aesthetics) 4. Art—Technique. I. Title.
N7680.J64 1989   743'.6   88-31084
ISBN 0-8306-5502-6

Design Press offers posters and The Cropper, a device for cropping artwork, for sale. For information, contact Mail-order Department. Design Press books are available at special discounts for bulk purchases for sales promotions, fund raisers, or premiums. For details contact Special Sales Manager. Questions regarding the content of the book should be addressed to:

Design Press
Division of TAB BOOKS Inc.
10 East 21 Street
New York, NY 10010

Contents

Acknowledgments

When embarking on a project like this, no one works in a vacuum. Friends help and people lend encouragement or expertise, and sometimes both. I owe a debt of gratitude to many—from my photo lab to my one-time boss at the ad agency, Maxine Moore, now a college English professor at the University of Missouri/Kansas City. Geologist R. J. Rudy read the chapter "Rocks and Other Geological Wonders" and offered his advice. Burt Wagenknecht, botanist at William Jewell College in Liberty, Missouri, read the chapters on plants and trees and kept me from making some major misstatements. Charles Newlon, biologist at Jewell, helped with the chapter on drawing animals.

Jim Weiser, the resident manager at the Martha Lafite Thompson Nature Sanctuary in Liberty, let me use his extensive library, answered questions, and allowed access at odd hours.

Roberta Hammer, friend and fellow artist, read over some chapters to make sure they were useful and concise.

If mistakes still appear in the text, they are *my* fault, not theirs. Mike Ward, editor at *The Artist's Magazine*, was unfailingly helpful, generous with his time, patient about deadlines. My other editors and art directors were understanding as well, and always willing to listen to the latest "progress report."

Charles W. Schwartz, the first wildlife artist whose work I was aware of, gave me a wonderful introduction to the field. His work is not only beautiful but accurate as well. Charlie has acted as mentor and guide-by-mail for years. Nancy Green, editorial director, mentor, friend, always there when I needed an answer, was supportive in the crucial stages.

All the artists whose work appears in these pages were generous to share their thoughts, drawings, and paintings.

I especially thank two fellow artist/naturalists for their encouragement as well as their more tangible help: Ann Zwinger and Clare Walker Leslie, both accomplished authors as well.

Finally, I thank my husband, Harris, always patient, always understanding (except, perhaps, about the dead shrew in the freezer waiting to be drawn).

Introduction

We all rush through our lives, in such a hurry to accomplish, to get through, to finish—what? Only our time on earth. We live vicariously through the media: television, movies, magazines, books—even the one you are holding! This book is intended not just as a peek at nature art, but as a tool, a key to help you see and live more fully.

Working from nature is more profound than simply producing pretty pictures to hang on someone's wall. It is a way of living, a healing. It is one way among many to be in touch with the core of reality that we all somehow know is there but which we are usually too busy to reach. That reality can be our center, our island of sanity in a sometimes crazy world. During a particularly difficult time of unemployment and stress in my own life, my field journal was the only thing that seemed to make sense. "In wildness is the preservation of the world," Henry David Thoreau wrote—he knew of the silences unbroken except by the chatter of a woodpecker, the whisper of leaves. He knew the feast of colors on an autumn day, the intricacy of the common weed. He had smelled the rich autumn scent of fallen leaves, the clean smell of sun-warmed grass, the musk of soil at a pond's edge. He knew the strength these things can bring us.

Thoreau kept journals; we can keep a field journal, a kind of naturalist's diary. We can experience firsthand the life of a weed or wildflower as we sit drawing it in the sun, and later our drawings and paintings can put us in touch once again with that abiding reality.

I can introduce you to some media and surfaces, such as pen-and-ink, watercolor, and scratchboard, and teach you some tricks of the trade. I can show you a bit about the laws of perspective and composition and explore with you some of the latest research on activity inherent in the right side of the brain as it affects creativity. But only nature can teach you to *see*. Nature and your own willingness to sit, to be still, to try and try again—willingness to fail, willingness to learn. Learning involves more than transforming nature into "art," capturing the magic of something live on paper or canvas. It is, in a way, becoming one with what you see, making it a part of your being. Leonardo da Vinci spoke of knowing how to see and said, "Because the eye can see, the soul is content to stay within the body." We will explore that seeing together.

In quiet, meditative drawing of a subject in nature, regardless of whether it is a weed, fungus, bird, or landscape, I learn much more than I ever do from a field guide. The weed becomes an individual plant, with its own personality and characteristics. It has a name, and the name, once learned, becomes a part of my experience in a way it never could from the more objective identification and classification in a book—facts soon forgotten. Perhaps in using the right side of the brain, the creative, responsive side, rather than the left, with its functions of reason and organization, learning becomes a personal—and pleasurable—response.

This book is about why to as well as how to draw and paint from nature. There are multitudes of how-to books on art, many of them excellent learning tools for technique and composition; and there are many good field guides and wildlife books. But working from life is almost like illustrating your own personal field guide. The *facts* can be looked up later in your Peterson's or Audubon, but the details, the life of what you draw and paint, impress themselves on your mind in a whole new way as you work.

Nature itself teaches us, inspires us, suggests myriad design possibilities. Many of my own works are studies, of leaves or birds or plants. They are "good" when I have slipped into a contemplative mood and have identified with the colors and shapes of my subject.

Drawing and painting from nature is not a way to gain entrance to the high-pressure art world, the world of changing fads, shows, and galleries. It is a way of living, and learning—and loving what you find along the way.

CHAPTER ONE

Tools and Supplies

1-1

B asic to any artistic expression are the tools used for that expression. Before you paint that oil or watercolor, before you execute that pen-and-ink or scratchboard drawing, before you build the subtle tones of pencil on your paper, you must first collect your chosen equipment. *What* you choose depends on a number of factors: will you create a piece of art, a finished and refined work meant to be framed and hung or perhaps reproduced, or do you simply want to keep a record of your experiences in nature in a kind of field journal? Do you have only a few minutes to spend, or have you set aside an afternoon, a day, a week for your painting or drawing? Will you work in your studio—however simply or completely equipped—or will you take your "studio" into the field? Planning, however spontaneous it may be, always forms the backbone of your work and precedes its success.

Pencils

The most basic and most immediate of tools for the artist is the pencil. It comes in many styles and degrees of hardness, from a 9H (hard) to a 6B (soft). You may prefer a simple no. 2 pencil from the local office-supply store. I most often use the middle range of hardnesses—HB, B, or 2B—since they allow a wide range of values from light to dark without the ex-cessive smudginess of the softer leads (Fig. 1-2). The harder leads are excellent for fine line work or scientific illustration where detail and line are all-important, but shading is difficult with them. In addition to smudging, the softer leads are difficult to keep sharply pointed and are best used for bold, broad effects.

If you work in the field often and do not wish to carry a lot of equipment, consider using a mechanical drawing pencil or leadholder. I use one with a 0.5mm lead that eliminates the need to carry a knife or other sharpener. These pencils take leads that are graded just as drawing pencils are. With a 2B lead, I can achieve a fairly satisfactory

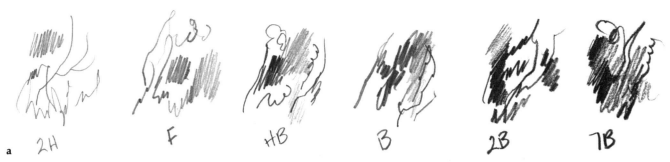

a   2H   F   HB   B   2B   7B

b

1-2. Pencils come in a variety of styles, with different hardnesses as well as lead qualities. (a) Test out several hardnesses to find the one most suited to your own style. The harder leads make a fine, clean line that tends to be a bit light in intensity, whereas the softest leads make dark lines that are subject to smudging. Pencils in the middle range are capable of making good darks while resisting smudging to some extent, but you may still want to spray them with a good fixative to protect your drawing. (b) You may wish to use a mechanical or technical pencil for in-the-field convenience, an artist's pencil, a regular no. 2 office pencil, or one of the specialty pencils such as a china marker. The pencil on the right is a woodless drawing pencil.

1-3. This drawing of a raccoon demonstrates the versatility and range possible with colored pencils. *Raccoon*, by Carol Sorensen, © 1984. Reproduced courtesy of the artist.

range of shaded values as well as a fine and sensitive line of sufficient blackness.

If you like the effect of charcoal but dislike the mess in the field, not to mention the tendency of the delicate sticks to break, try a charcoal pencil. This is a versatile medium with a variety of applications.

You may want to experiment with colored pencils as well. They have a waxy base, do not smear as regular pencils do, reproduce well, and are often used for illustrations (Fig. 1-3). They offer a highly portable, nonmessy way of transporting color to the field; in the studio, where there is room to spread out, color choices are almost unlimited. On the debit side, they are difficult to sharpen without breaking the lead. (A single-edge razor blade may prove most useful.)

Pen-and-Ink

With pen-and-ink, the line you draw is very nearly "set in stone." It can be as expressive and delicate as a spider's web, as bold and decisive as a piece of abstract art. Every hesitation, every mistake in judgment, every mood swing is exposed there in black-and-white—as telling as a line drawn by a lie detector's needle! It is more permanent than a pencil drawing, which can be erased, changed, redrawn. The stark black lines on white paper are *you*.

In drawing from nature, pen-and-ink must be used with care. It is not appropriate for all subjects: the technique and the particular drawing tool must be well matched to the subject itself. It does, however, reproduce beautifully.

A wide variety of pens and nibs are available, capable of achieving myriad effects (Fig. 1-4). A simple crow-quill pen is inexpensive and capable of a number of expressions, from a fine tracing of the

1-4. The variety of pens available offers a broad range of line. (a) This sample of lines drawn by dip pens shows only a few of the effects that can be achieved. A crow-quill pen makes very fine lines. Regular drawing nibs come in a variety of sizes; the sample shown here is a B-6 nib, the smallest round nib you can buy. You may prefer a pointed drawing nib. A bamboo pen is unpredictable and does not hold a lot of ink but makes beautiful spontaneous marks. A calligraphy pen will give you unusual effects. (b) A few of the pens you may want to try include, from left to right, a fine-pointed felt-tipped pen; a 2×0 technical pen; a fountain pen; a crow-quill pen; a hawk-quill pen; a dip pen with a round nib; a bamboo pen; and a black ball-point. Notice the various strokes possible with each pen.

contours of a plant to a densely built-up area of crosshatched lines used to depict a forest.

You can buy drawing nibs in a number of styles and sizes, from points as small as a crow-quill's to a huge nib of multiple metal strips normally used for calligraphy. It is not necessary to limit yourself only to the pointed drawing nibs—the flat ones of various widths intended for lettering

000
Technical
Pen

#3
Technical
Pen

Pelikan
Sketch Pen

Black
Ball-point
pen

1-5. You may prefer a pen that carries its own ink supply for work in the field, such as one of those shown here: technical pens of two sizes, a sketch-type pen, and a black ball-point. Your choice will depend on personal preference and the effect you want to achieve.

make interesting accents. Round and oval nibs may be useful in overcoming a certain pen-and-ink spikiness or for conveying a bolder, stronger mood.

Bamboo pens come in a number of sizes, some with a watercolor brush on the opposite end. Flexibility varies somewhat, and they do not hold a lot of ink, but they make such a nice, unique mark that their shortcomings are easily forgiven. They can be altered or trimmed with a pocketknife if they become broken or worn. They can be used with any ink or with liquid dye watercolor, which adheres well to the porous wooden nibs.

These pens all require an open bottle of ink, making them perhaps more suitable for studio than field work. For sketching outdoors, consider a fountain-type sketch pen or a technical pen (Fig. 1-5). Sketch pens often have expressive, flexible nibs, allowing a range of effects from a delicate, fine line to one of bold Oriental simplicity. A good sketch pen is well worth the money it costs (be-

tween eight and fifteen dollars, generally).

For even, uniform lines of predetermined width, try a technical pen (Fig. 1-6). These come in a variety of point sizes, from a tiny 6 × 0 to a hefty no. 7. They work by means of a fine wire that moves up and down in an only slightly larger metal tube, regulating the flow of ink. The size of the tube determines the width of your line. The key to using these wonderful, frustrating pens, capable of mak-

ing such clean, uniform lines, is maintenance. If ink dries in the tube, the pen must be dismantled according to the manufacturer's directions and cleaned. I have a threaded rubber bulb that holds pen cleaner or warm water, and almost as a matter of course, I first unscrew the pen-point section and screw it onto the bulb to force water or solution through the tip before beginning to work. Use only ink formulated for technical pens; the higher varnish content of other inks may clog the delicate mechanism. Warnings aside, if you are willing to work within the requirements (and temper fits) of these pens, you may produce some of your best work. Again, these reproduce beautifully.

You can use any ink with dip pens. My favorite is a sepia ink (brown) that gives a softness and subtlety difficult to achieve with the black inks. It is particularly suited to drawings of wildlife, but not if the drawings are intended for reproduction (good-quality, dense black ink must be used for that purpose). Buy a good brand of ink, whatever color you choose, even if you do not intend your work for print. Some cheaper inks vary so much in quality that whole passages of a drawing may look grayed.

You may want to try drawing with a good-quality ball-point

1-6. This drawing was done with a technical pen on a very smooth (plate) paper. Lines of uniform width can be achieved with this paper, since there is very little tooth to affect the pen's nib or ink flow. *Douglas Fir with Cone*, by Cathy Johnson. Reproduced courtesy of the Kansas City, Missouri, Board of Parks and Recreation Commissioners.

pen. They can be purchased anywhere, of course, but art-supply stores carry some with special drawing ink. These make a line almost as expressive as that of a pencil, with a subtlety not possible with other ink pens. Keep a tissue handy for the occasional blob that forms on the tip—check the point before you touch it to your paper. Some inks may fade eventually to a warm brown—nice in itself, but not if you wanted a dark black line.

Brushes

When buying paintbrushes get the best you can afford. Fighting a limp, shedding brush is a curse no one should have to bear! If you do not want the expense of red sable for watercolor or boar bristle for oils, try some of the new synthetics or mixtures of synthetic or natural bristles. Painter and teacher John Pike recommended ox hair for watercolor and did some wonderful paintings using these less expensive brushes.

Try out watercolor brushes with clean water before you buy them, to test for springiness and good point. Better art-supply stores will have a container of water near the brush display or will find one if you request it. You have to live and work with your brushes, and you are paying for them, so do not be embarrassed about asking to test them.

As Figure 1-7 shows, watercolor brushes are generally either round (pointed) or flat (squared). Buy the biggest round with a good point that you can afford (and these *are* expensive). It will hold enough water and pigment for a generous wash but still be capable of fine detail. Supplement if you wish with one or two smaller brushes, perhaps a no. 2 and a no. 6 or no. 7, but try the bigger one first. A tiny brush practically guarantees overworking unless you are using a very small format.

1-7. Try out different kinds of brushes to see what works best for a specific purpose. This photo includes, from left to right, two round watercolor brushes, two flats or lettering brushes, a fan brush, a rigger, and an old stenciling brush. All are useful in evoking nature.

Flats were once used only by sign painters, but watercolorists and designers have discovered the delightful range of strokes possible with these brushes. They have great versatility and, like the large round brush, will help prevent too tight an approach. Happily, these are also considerably cheaper than rounds, and the mixtures of synthetic and natural hairs are quite satisfactory. I most often use a ½-inch, a ¾-inch, and a 1-inch brush and find them very useful for landscape work. A larger 1½-inch flat or house-painting brush comes in handy for broad washes.

You may wish to try some of the specialty brushes (see Fig. 1-7). The riggers (also known as liners) make wonderfully unpredictable, sweeping, dancing lines, great for tree branches, vines, tall weeds, and grasses. Fan brushes can be used to depict bare trees in winter, distant trees on a hill, or grasses waving in the hot August sun.

Use a stenciling brush or old toothbrush for spatter. The effect is loose and free and gives a nice texture to earth or weathered wood. See chapter 3 for suggestions on technique.

These brushes are not the only tools that can be used with paint; see chapter 3 for ideas on other painting tools.

Oil or acrylic brushes are not discussed herein, except in passing, since those media are not covered in this book. My blanket advice still stands, however—buy the best you can and use the largest brush you can, for as *long* as you can, before graduating to a smaller brush.

Paints

Here again, buy the best you can afford. A set of child's pan-type watercolors may be sufficient to discover if you like water-base media, but for any serious use, graduate as quickly as possible.

Art-supply stores carry a selection of good pan colors, if you prefer that type, or tube colors for quick and easy mixing. Tube colors will dry on your palette but can be refreshed with water just as pan colors can.

You will want a good selection of primary colors (red, yellow, and blue), generally a warm and a cool version of each plus a few good earth colors for mixing browns and grays. See chapter 3 for a more complete listing of suggested pigments.

Gouache is an opaque watercolor that is used by many outdoor artists, commercial artists, illustrators, and designers. If you want to experiment with the effect before investing in a set of colors, mix a bit of white gouache with each of your regular tube watercolors to make them opaque. If you decide you like the effect, invest in a good set of *permanent* gouache. (Be sure to check for lightfastness. Some, intended for illustration only, fade rapidly.)

1-9. This scratchboard drawing is much more intricate than most. The artist supplements normal scratchboard tools with a needle for fine work. Untitled, by Lee Salber. Reproduced courtesy of the artist.

1-8. I enjoy working on butcher paper or other toned paper, as it provides built-in subtle halftone effects. This sketch was executed with a razor-pointed felt-tipped pen and a white Prismacolor pencil, using the warm tan of the paper as the middle value. Light-struck areas were indicated with the white pencil, giving a range of values to the drawing with a minimum of equipment. *Jonquils*, by Cathy Johnson. Reproduced courtesy of *The Artist's Magazine*.

Surfaces

The surface you choose depends on the effect you are trying to achieve. A simple bond (typing) paper of good quality may be less intimidating than the more expensive art papers to begin with or for practice or rough planning. It is fine for pencil or ink drawings but too lightweight for watercolor washes.

Watercolor papers are graded by weight—which is based on the scale weight of 500 sheets of that paper. The 70-pound or 90-pound paper is good for drawings or for a very dry application of watercolor unless you plan to prestretch it; 140-pound paper is my favorite weight, as it will take washes with minimal buckling. Paper that is 300 pounds or heavier will take very wet washes with no problems but is quite expensive.

Paper comes in various tooths or textures, which can be exploited according to your needs. Paper is designated as hot press, sometimes called smooth or plate, which is good for ink or technical work; cold press, a paper with a bit of texture; or rough—which can be very rough indeed. Vellum-finish bristol has a surface texture excellent for pencil, ink, pastels, colored pencils, or other media. Some papers can be bought in grays, tans, and a range of colors. I like to work on butcher paper for the warm middle tones it affords (Fig. 1-8). Some artists even have this paper bound into sketchbooks! Unlike the better drawing and painting surfaces, however, this paper is wood-pulp based and highly acidic rather than having a neutral pH as many artists' papers do. Its acidity causes it to become brittle with age, so I seldom use it for serious work. For those I want to last, I buy a good brand of toned paper.

Scratchboard and coquille board are two surfaces that can be very useful for certain effects (Figs. 1-9, 1-10, 1-11, and 1-12). Scratchboard

pencil drawing
transferred to scratchboard

inked-in where you
want darks — outline in-
cluded

scratch away details &
highlights

1-10. Scratchboard is basically very simple to use as a rendering surface, as this start-to-finish drawing shows. Any good art-supply store should have scratchboard (sometimes called scraper board) in several weights. You can also buy a pre-inked board if the majority of your drawing is to be black.

1-11. I used coquille board and a black china marker for this landscape drawing.

is a clay-coated surface, either pre-inked with black or left white; I prefer the white surface for most projects, since I can place my darks where I want them. The ink is allowed to dry thoroughly on the surface, then scratched or scraped with special tools for a white-on-black effect. Be sure to look for professional-quality scratchboard with a good, thick coating of fine clay; student-grade scratchboard is frustrating and will not produce smooth lines when incised. Because of the manipulation and scraping of the surface, scratchboard drawings may not be suitable for framing, but these imperfections disappear in photoreproduction.

Coquille board has a lightly textured surface that allows you to create shades of gray easily. It is not pH balanced (acid free), so a drawing done on this surface will not last as long as one done on archival-quality surfaces. Because halftone *effects* can be reproduced

1-12. This stipple-board drawing exhibits effects similar to those produced by drawing on coquille board. The textured surface lends itself to halftone effects, even if you are using a black china marker or litho pencil. Accents can be added with black ink if desired. *Tapir*, by Carolyn Rathbun.

from a coquille-board rendering without the necessity of actually screening for halftone, it is a useful tool for the illustrator as well.

A bit of practice with coquille board is all that is necessary to create interesting effects. The amount of pressure applied to a black china marker or litho crayon affects the density of tone, as the

1-13. An eraser shield is a useful tool in watercolor painting as well as drawing. Not only will it protect your drawing when erasing, but it can be used as a tool to lift lights where you want to recapture the white of your paper.

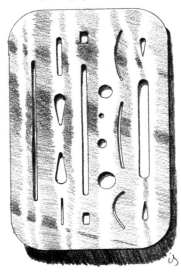

raised texture of the surface is covered and the indentations fill with pigment. You may wish to use a true flat black for accents by adding india ink.

If you are working outdoors, you will need a hard working surface. You may solve that problem by using a simple bound sketchbook with a heavy cardboard backing, a watercolor block (paper bound on four sides with an access point to free successive paintings), or a Masonite or lightweight plywood board slightly bigger than your sheet of paper.

Other Tools

Additional tools you may need or want include the following.

Erasers: Filmar White Magic or another vinyl eraser, kneaded eraser, soft pink eraser, or one in pencil form (I prefer the Filmar White Magic since it does not abrade the paper). I have recently discovered a handy retractable mechanical-pencil type of eraser made of white vinyl that is ideal for field work.

Eraser shield (Fig. 1-13): this protects the rest of your drawing from inadvertent disappearance and allows control in tight spaces.

It can also be used as a drawing tool.

Army canteen (Fig. 1-14): for carrying water to the field. The cup can be used for mixing watercolors (a well-rinsed plastic bleach jug will do as well).

Portable plastic palette: experiment to find the type that suits you best—I like my John Pike model with a lid for easy transport.

You may prefer a metal watercolorist's kit with pigments and mixing wells all in one—extremely portable.

Not strictly art supplies, the following tools will be handy working in the field—especially if you find your interest as artist/naturalist growing (Fig. 1-15):

- binoculars
- pocket microscope
- hand lens (Fig. 1-16)
- 16-inch plastic ruler marked in inches and centimeters
- small viewfinder cut from lightweight cardboard or 3-inch by 5-inch card to help you frame possible compositions
- pocketknife for sharpening pencils or collecting small samples
- pencil sharpener, if desired

Do not overload yourself. Be selective when buying tools (keep them as lightweight as possible for field work) and when packing up for a field trip. You will not need *everything* on every trip, and you can complete your work at home or in the studio where everything is at hand.

Packing Up

The supplies to bring to sketch in the field depend to some degree on how long you will be away from your studio. In most cases you will be a short driving distance from home, and ordinary supplies will do fine: your field journal or sketchbook, felt-tipped pens, pencils or colored pencils, or

1-14. An old army canteen makes a perfect water container. The canteen nests in a cup that holds clean water conveniently. You do not always know if you will be working near water or if nearby water will be drinkable, so a canteen is a useful addition to a field setup.

1-15. Handy equipment for field study includes field guides on various subjects (birds, flowers, trees, shells, tracks, butterflies), binoculars, drawing equipment, hand lens, field microscope, spiral or hardbound sketchbook, and a 6-inch ruler, plus a knapsack, hat, insect repellent, thermos, what-have-you.

small watercolor kit and container of clean water.

For a longer, day trip or a sketching vacation, you should plan as carefully as you otherwise do when traveling. You will not want to break the mood, lose the light, or ruin the day by having to hike back to the car and drive somewhere for that forgotten or overlooked item.

Your personal checklist depends on how you like to work. Media and size are important considerations. I usually work in watercolor; if you work in pastels, pen-and-ink, oils, acrylics, or other media, your supplies will differ somewhat from those that follow.

My largest in-the-field drawings are usually about 9 by 12 inches, but I have done pieces as large as half-sheet watercolors, 15 by 22 inches, outdoors. Larger works require special materials. I have a Masonite board with two large clips that can carry several half-sheets of watercolor paper. This can be slipped into a large canvas

envelope with carrying straps for easy handling and protection from the elements.

A knapsack holds the rest of my supplies (when I work with a 9- by 12-inch or smaller sketchbook or watercolor block, the Masonite

1-16. A hand lens is helpful if you need to draw tiny details of plants, flowers, bugs, and other small plants and animals. More modern versions than this one, which was my grandfather's, have up to three degrees of magnification, depending on how many lenses of varying powers you use.

board is dispensed with altogether). The knapsack contains: paper (sketchbook, journal, or watercolor block); watercolor brushes rolled in a bamboo placemat to protect their bristles; a small traveling watercolor box with paints; several drawing pencils; a razor-pointed felt-tipped pen or sketching pen; a selection of colored pencils in a pencil container; a pencil sharpener, knife, or sandpaper block; a supply of clean water in an old canteen; masking tape if I have brought my Masonite board and loose sheets of watercolor paper; and tissues or paper towels.

Remember that man does not live by art supplies alone—or we would have a lot *more* starving artists. If you plan to spend some time at work, take lunch and beverage.

A foam pad to sit on, especially if you plan to draw in a particularly rocky place for any length of time, or a piece of plastic or tarp if the ground is damp, will help ensure your comfort. You can

1-17. This mourning-cloak butterfly, drawn in late winter, was as chilly as I was.

1-18. This park was drawn from a snow-covered deck overlooking it. Such a protected location allows you to work outdoors in winter in relative comfort. Many artists find working in their cars in winter a good alternative to the warmth of the studio. *Deck*, by Keith Hammer. Reproduced courtesy of the artist.

work longer—and better—if you eliminate as many distractions as possible.

A hat shades your eyes and your paper from the sun's glare in summer; in winter a cap may make the difference in comfort. You may even want to try "fingerless" gloves from a sporting goods store, and insect repellent is essential in many locales.

Many artists seem to feel that, once the riot of colors in autumn has gone, it is time to forget about working directly from nature until spring's renaissance comes around. Not so. With a little planning—plus some care for creature comforts—the glacial blues of a forbidding snowdrift, the black lace of winter limbs against the sky, the startling red of rosehips and cardinals against the snow, the first stirrings of new life in late winter can serve as fascinating subjects as well (Fig. 1-17).

Dress appropriately, and protect your drawing supplies against rough weather. Wear down- or polyester-filled clothing, wool socks, and waterproof boots, plus a head covering on cold days (a great deal of the body's heat escapes from the head, especially noticeable when you stand still to sketch). John Pike used to take a

bit of alcohol along to keep his paint water from freezing in winter (it kept his fingers supple too).

For the truly devoted, on wet days it is possible to hold a small sketchbook and both your hands inside a clear plastic bag and draw without ruining your paper. Some artists take an entire portable studio in the form of a traveling easel and other accoutrements, but since I often climb to where I plan to work, I like to carry my supplies on my back and keep my hands free. I wear lots of pockets for the same reason. These come in handy in the winter too. When it is really cold, I can do a quick habitat sketch or small landscape on the spot and then carry small items home in my pockets to sketch later. You can also work in a sheltered area outdoors, which provides some measure of comfort (Fig. 1-18).

Whatever you pack, keep your checklist handy to be sure you have everything you need next time. Add or delete items as necessary. Simplify if you can—that stuff gets heavy! And, most important, remember that whatever you unpack in the field must be repacked when you leave. The old wilderness adage "Take noth-

1-20. Transparent watercolor was used in this study of leaves and berries. Untitled, by Peggy McKeehan. Reproduced courtesy of the artist.

ing but pictures, leave nothing but footprints" applies to artists as well.

A Simple Setup

If you find gathering all these tools and supplies a little overwhelming, you can use a much simpler setup and still produce satisfying drawings. If you become a professional artist, your list of necessary supplies will grow like Topsy. But if you would simply like to learn, to begin experiencing firsthand the world around you, or to enjoy a few moments of drawing in nature, keep your supplies simple. Take a no. 2 pencil, with a sharpener if you like (or carry a mechanical pencil and dispense with the sharpener), a clipboard, and several sheets of good typing paper with you. If you like, substitute a small sketchbook (no larger than 9 by 12 inches). People in less equipment-conscious countries than ours make do with even less, drawing on scraps of paper, backs of envelopes, whatever is available. Some of my own favorite

1-21. Scratchboard and ink worked well in creating the portrait of this showy blackbird. *Yellow-headed Blackbird*, by Lee Salber. Reproduced courtesy of the artist.

1-19. Pen-and-ink was used to create this sensitive study of a sticky monkey flower. *Diplacus*, by Marianne D. Wallace. Reproduced courtesy of the artist.

TOOLS AND SUPPLIES 19

1-22. A lithographer's pencil was used to capture the moment of "Strike!" in this print of a big old lunker. *Lily Pad Bass*, by Ernest Lussier. Reproduced courtesy of the artist.

quick sketches have been done with just such handy supplies. That is how I discovered the pleasant subtleties of ball-point pens for sketching—I had nothing else with me at the time. The same can be said for razor-pointed felt-tipped pens—if that is what you have with you, never mind that they are not considered good-quality equipment—use them. Do not let the lack of "proper" equipment keep you from recording a special moment.

A Field Journal

To have a more permanent record of your experiences in nature, as well as a place for planning and dreaming, you may wish to keep a field journal or naturalist's sketchbook, and this is covered in detail in chapter 9. Any sketchbook of a portable size will do; I find the most convenient spiral-bound book is 6½ by 9 inches. It is small enough to fit in a backpack or to be carried by hand. You may prefer a larger size, but I can do loose landscape studies or detailed drawings in the smaller size, while maintaining portability. This size is less obtrusive too—a large sketchbook flapping about in a breeze will frighten off all but the most stoic of wildlife subjects!

A good hardbound sketchbook makes the best permanent field journal. It can withstand a lot of abuse in the field (I have dropped mine over a cliff, with only a scuffed corner to show for it), and the hard binding provides a built-in drawing support. On my usual morning ramble, I most frequently use my hardbound sketchbook and my 0.5mm mechanical pencil with 2B lead, but at home in my studio, tools and supplies of course tend to get somewhat more complicated. You too will use your own special tools at home and abroad as you begin to work and experience drawing and painting from nature.

CHAPTER TWO

The Basics

2-1

We are so attuned to jumping in and getting started in this hurry-up world that we tend to carry this same attitude into working from nature. Of course, we all lead busy lives, and time to go out and draw or paint *is* sometimes literally snatched from other duties and occupations. But often we pursue *all* our activities at this same breakneck pace, to their detriment and our great loss. Part of the wonder of working from nature derives from taking time: time to experience it fully, time to get to know that particular bird or bug or vista, time to allow it to become a part of us. When you go out to draw, take a little time for planning and dreaming. Be still—do not fidget and thrash about.

Stop. Let the serenity around you begin to soak in. Take some time for discovery.

Planning

One of the hardest things for me to do when drawing or painting is to stop *thinking*—or perhaps I should say to stop reacting to learned responses. When we are children, we are taught that grass is green, sky is blue, earth is brown, and daisies are white. We learn that a shape rather like a lollipop—round and green on top with a brown stick—represents a tree and water is a blue streak across our paper. But before we "learned our colors" with the help of endless books and

rainbow-hued blocks, we *saw* the colors. We marveled at the shapes of things in all their wonderful variety. We saw everything, fresh, new, and without the barrier of learned symbols. To draw nature we need to return to the wonder and freshness of a child. We need to open our eyes, quit *naming* things to ourselves, and react to what is there, not to what we have been taught.

Trees are not simply green. There are shades and values of greens, shiny leaves and dull leaves, leaves that absorb the light on hairy surfaces, leaves that reflect the blue of the sky, leaves that glow with golden light when sunlight passes through them—a phenomenon that must have inspired the first stained glass. Some leaves yellow as they die, some have red pigments in their leaves as the chlorophyll dissipates. Trees are short and gnarled, tall and stately, or full of delightfully unexpected angles like a sycamore. They may resemble an exclamation point or a woman's flowing hair. Look. See what is really there before you. If you need to, spend a moment or two getting your mind and heart and spirit set, allowing your creative self, the right side of your brain, to take over.

For me, drawing from nature is a wonderful excuse to do what I love most—to escape to the quiet but lively world outside my door, far from phone and deadlines and responsibilities. I explore my small piece of the world, and I dream and search and simply sit in wonder. I become a child again, sitting in the mud by the Fishing River. I watch the workings of frogs not much bigger than my thumbnail

2-2. "Image," or envision, your drawing on your paper before you begin, to make sure it is well placed. I used this technique to help plan the correct angles between my cat and the edges of the paper, to gain pleasing negative shapes and proper perspective.

and collect tiny snail shells with a child's delight in the miniature. Even with my sharpest lead, I could not begin to draw them life-size in all their tiny perfection. My ruler shows they are less than ⅜ inch long.

Only after I have taken a little time to experience my environment am I ready to draw. I will have become calm; I will have been able to envision which of the myriad possibilities around me I will choose for a subject. Dreaming can become reality.

This step is a natural outgrowth of planning and dreaming. After I have chosen my subject, I spend a moment or two just *looking* at it before I begin to draw. Of course, if it is a nervous, scolding squirrel or a circling vulture, I will not be able to count on it staying still for long, if at all. But even if it moves, the moment spent in quiet observation will have helped me fix the image in my mind. I may still be able to transfer it successfully to paper. Many athletes are using a new technique in training that artists may find equally useful—it is, in fact, one that artists have used unconsciously for ages, but psychologists have only recently given it a name. The athlete imagines himself going through every step of his performance—what he will do, how he will do it, how he will feel. The technique is called *imaging,* and it works as well in the fine arts. "Image" your drawing onto your paper before you begin drawing (Fig. 2-2).

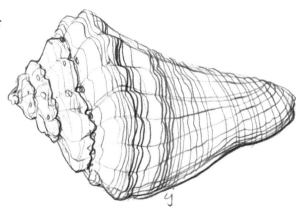

2-3. Both outer contour and internal volume can be expressed only with line and pencil pressure.

Where will you place the head in relation to the paper's edge—and in relation to the back or paw or tail? If the animal moves, you will have that image in your mind's eye, an invaluable aid in capturing the constantly moving natural world. Even those subjects that do not move are easier to get down on paper with a little creative imaging. After all, you still must decide where to place a petal or a mountain range on the flat plane of the paper.

The things that we see leave an imprint on our minds that can be recalled almost like calling up data on a computer. The shape of a black vulture as it flies overhead and disappears beyond the hill is still there, in your mind, which is, after all, the original and most magnificent computer. Simply being still and recalling what we have seen can become a highly developed skill, invaluable to the artist. It is wonderful to be able to draw or paint something that stays obediently before you, but much of nature is obedient only to itself, as it should be. We can adapt to this constant change by disciplining our eyes, our mind. It only takes a bit of practice plus a belief that it is possible.

Loosening Up

You may want to make a few very light pencil strokes on your paper to position your drawing on the page. These lines will disappear later under the completed work—

or will form an interesting vibration if they occur outside of the final line. Many artists do a kind of quick phantom drawing, moving their pencil rapidly over the paper without touching it as a kind of planning exercise that also helps them loosen up. Try moving more than just your fingers—do not hold them tightly about the pencil as if about to write. Loosen your grip somewhat, and use your wrist and forearm in the movement. Let your elbow work a bit too. If you are working with a large format, you may be able to use your whole arm to create sweeping, loose lines that will take on authority and confidence. *Then* you can tighten back up to do a very detailed drawing if you wish.

Contour Drawing

Many artists recommend contour drawing as a way to capture what they see less self-consciously but with a kind of inner integrity. There are a number of ways to do contour drawing. Some people suggest drawing quickly, the pencil never leaving the paper's surface, while looking only at the subject and never at your paper. Others suggest a minimum of "peeking," but with a slow, careful tracing of the contour as if your pencil were actually touching the subject itself. You may want to glance down as you change direction to check positioning on the page or general relationships of parts within the drawing.

In Figure 2-3, I obviously looked at the paper as well as the subject, but I allowed my pencil to describe the roundness of the shell as well as its spiral qualities. I pretended I was drawing on the shell itself, feeling the bumps and curves and contours with my point as I went. Figure 2-4 is closer to pure contour drawing. It was executed by looking at only my subject, preventing any overcon-

2-4. Try doing a modified contour drawing. In this sample I looked down only as I neared the end of the drawing, to connect the starting and ending points. This technique is useful in freeing yourself of too much concern for the finished product and in gaining familiarity with the subject. The resulting drawing is often quite beautiful and free.

cern with perfection on my part. As I neared my starting point, I looked down at the paper to check only that the lines connected at the end.

Try both of these methods to see which best helps you become involved in your drawing. Perhaps pure contour drawing might be a way to shift gears into a kind of altered drawing state at the beginning of a session, as suggested by Betty Edwards in her book *Drawing on the Right Side of the Brain*.

Take a sheet of paper (typing paper will do), and fasten it somehow to your drawing surface so it stays in place. With a sharp-pointed pencil or ball-point or felt-tipped pen, start drawing the form at any point—wherever it seems comfortable for you. I usually start somewhere in the upper left and work clockwise, but if you are left-handed, you may choose just the opposite. Looking only (or mostly) at your subject, begin to trace the outline

on your paper. Do not lift the pencil to draw details inside the subject, or you will become hopelessly lost; "draw into" the form, then return to the outline. Painter Charles Reid also suggests drawing out into the background to integrate your subject more fully with its surroundings. If you want, look at your paper when you make a major change in direction, but not otherwise. The image you draw will have a kind of life you might not have achieved in more tentative, belabored, or self-conscious drawing. The pleasure in this kind of exercise is that you cannot expect your finished product to have the kind of perfection or refinement you usually expect of yourself. There is no way to be disappointed with the results since, for the most part, you were not even looking at the paper. It is the special beauty of these works that is so often an unexpected—and very pleasant—result. And contour drawing cer-

2-5. An HB pencil was used on smooth paper to give this drawing a sense of life. The piece appeared in Ann Zwinger's book *A Desert Country Near the Sea*, published by Harper and Row in 1983. Pencil drawing, by Ann Zwinger. Reproduced courtesy of the artist.

tainly enables you to see what is before you, to pay attention to it rather than fussing over the finished product.

Pencil Drawing

As mentioned, pencil drawing is the most basic of all forms of artistic impression. A pencil drawing can be a simple line drawing, as in a contour drawing, or it can be as detailed as you wish. Many people think of a pencil drawing only as a *sketch*, something to be used as a study for something

2-6. Pressure on the pencil's lead was varied as the point followed the ins and outs of this fossilized turtle shell.

else—a means to an end. It can be that and more.

Many of the illustrations in this book are pencil drawings; some obviously were done as quick studies or field sketches; some are works of art in themselves. Ann Zwinger, nature writer and artist, does sensitive, elegant pencil drawings that are in the latter category (Fig. 2-5). They do not need to ''become'' anything else. Many nineteenth-century American artists did incredibly complete pencil drawings, either as ends in themselves or as studies for large oil paintings. They used these works to show the ''civilized'' world back east what the raw, powerful country in the west looked like, or to compile field studies for natural history uses. Charles Herbert Moore, Albert Bierstadt, Asher B. Durand, Frances Anne Hopkins, and George Caleb Bingham are among those who explored their environment with pencil in hand.

When drawing with pencil, try using different pressures on the lead to create varied lines with more interesting effect (Fig. 2-6). One artist of my acquaintance

uses a darker line where elements meet, accentuating the turnings of a leaf or the joining of a petal. Clare Walker Leslie, artist and author of several books, suggests using the heaviest lines to express those elements nearest the viewer, as in a petal or leaf that points toward you.

This same principle can work with shaded areas in drawing landscapes in pencil. Those areas in the foreground (or nearest you) can be darkest, as well as the most detailed; the middle ground is suggested by the middle gray tones; and the background becomes pale and relatively undetailed as it fades into the distance (Fig. 2-7). Try doing a landscape drawing using only three line widths or weights to express this kind of distance instead of using shaded areas. Try three pencils (soft, medium, and hard) to achieve this effect visually. You may produce a beautiful, expressive (if unexpected) drawing.

Experiment with line widths and strokes to see what you might use to express different things. Leaves can be depicted in a quick, dark scribble, darker still in the

2-7. Distance and atmosphere can be suggested with lead pressure. This landscape sketch expresses depth through the use of darks and lights created by varying lead pressure and pencil hardness.

shadowed areas, or with a number of short, choppy strokes with a wide lead. Fur might be rendered with a heavier stroke, becoming lighter and thinner as you reduce pressure on the lead to suggest the direction of hair growth or the light source (Fig. 2-8).

For a very detailed pencil drawing with little or no shading, a relatively hard lead, well sharpened, can be ideal. A bold landscape with thunderous darks is best expressed using the width of the lead and a softer pencil.

A tortillon or a stump (rolled, pointed tubes of paper, available at art-supply stores) may be used to blend areas of shading. Technical illustrators often use carbon or graphite dust applied with a sable brush, stump or tortillon to capture the subtle shading of their subjects. Try the following technique using dust from your pencil. With a soft lead pencil, make a number of heavy strokes on a piece of scrap paper. Pick up the dust with your stump and apply it where you want soft shading on your drawing. Before you touch the loaded stump or tortillon to your paper, tap lightly to remove excess dust to avoid blobs or too-heavy areas.

2-8. Charles W. Schwartz is expert at rendering fur with a pencil. Look closely to see how his overlapping strokes capture the look and feel of the rabbit's fur. *Eastern Cottontail*, by Charles W. Schwartz. Reproduced courtesy of the artist, the Conservation Commission of the State of Missouri, the University of Missouri Press, and the State Historical Society of Missouri.

I experimented with this technique on my drawing of a hapless opossum that had the misfortune to become trapped in my compost barrel (Fig. 2-9). I found the tortillon technique useful in depicting the softness of his gray fur.

Pencil drawings can be altered or enhanced in a number of ways. An eraser can be a tool for *making* drawings as well as fixing mistakes. Along with an eraser shield, an eraser can be used to pick fine lines out of a shaded area to highlight leaf veins, fur, light-struck limbs, or mountaintops. A kneaded eraser can be molded to a sharp point to pick out highlights in much the same way.

It is necessary to use a paper with good tooth for pencil drawings. This means that the paper's surface has tiny depressions that catch and hold the graphite on the page. A too-slick paper will simply fight you, making lines appear too light.

A soft lead in the wrong hands

2-9. This opossum was drawn using a graphite dust technique similar to that used by scientific illustrators. Graphite dust was applied with a tortillon, then longer guard hairs were rendered in pencil. Straight pencil technique was used in the close-up studies of feet and tail.

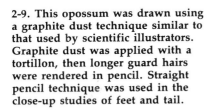

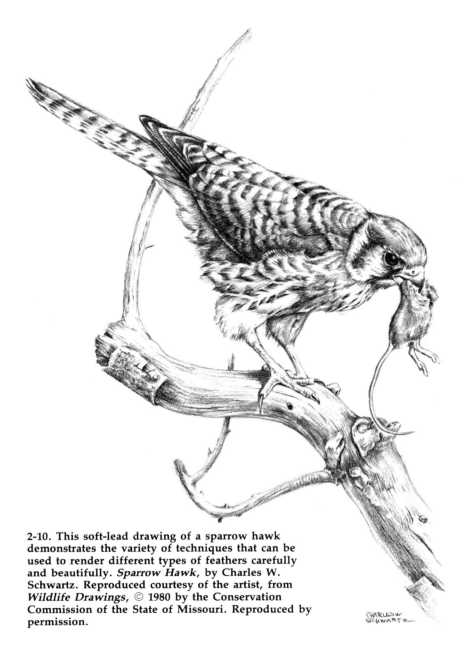

2-10. This soft-lead drawing of a sparrow hawk demonstrates the variety of techniques that can be used to render different types of feathers carefully and beautifully. *Sparrow Hawk*, by Charles W. Schwartz. Reproduced courtesy of the artist, from *Wildlife Drawings*, © 1980 by the Conservation Commission of the State of Missouri. Reproduced by permission.

drawing, as all parts of it will be done at approximately the same stage. You still must avoid dragging the piece of paper over the drawing's surface so as not to smear your work, of course. Perhaps the best solution for smudges is Andrew Wyeth's—when doing pencil sketches, he simply does not worry about them. (I never mind them on his work, only on my own!)

Keeping a clean piece of paper under your drawing hand is also a good idea if you are doing an ink drawing or sketching in details to be painted later in watercolor—or use fingerless gloves to protect the paper. Oil from your hands can be deposited on the paper, making smooth adherence of ink or paint difficult.

Pen-and-Ink

A wide range of pens and nibs is available. Try to match your choice to your subject matter and technique for best results. A fine-pointed technical pen can create a very beautiful wildlife or botanical drawing, as it can perfectly capture tiny details, the delicate way a leaf joins a stem or the intricacies of a bird's feathers. This was my tool of choice for a series of botanicals done for the R. L. Sweet Arboretum in Kansas City, and I was happy with the resulting simple but expressive drawings (Fig. 2-11). A bolder sketch pen with a flexible nib is good for landscapes or for drawing animals, and a wide-nibbed calligraphy pen can be fun to use to make an almost abstract interpretation of an outdoor scene.

If I find my drawings getting too precious with tiny details, I switch to a round-nibbed pen and experiment with broader, more graphic effects (Fig. 2-12). Look at the works of Eskimo or American Indian artists. The simple, strong lines of Inuit art may point you in a new direction.

can produce a messy drawing, not to mention a gray smudge up the arm. For those who want to employ the effects only a soft pencil can produce (Fig. 2-10), a few tricks can be used to minimize this mess. First, use soft leads to do quick, bold sketches, preferably from a standing position, and with a sweeping motion of the hand and arm so your hand never rests on the paper to smear it in the first place. If you like the rich darks afforded by the softer leads but want to use a more detailed approach, you can start in the up-

per left corner of your page and work diagonally down and across your paper (if you are right-handed; lefties, work from the upper right) so you never drag graphite from one area to another. Try keeping a clean piece of paper under the hand resting on the drawing; it allows you to work the entire drawing at once and keep it going at an even pace compositionally, rather than working strictly from left to right. You can keep better track of it that way, and your technique will not change halfway through the

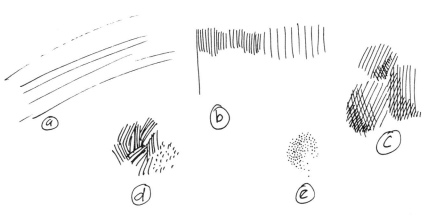

2-11. A 2×0 technical pen was used to do this careful rendering for the R.L. Sweet Arboretum in Kansas City, Missouri. *White Pine*, by Cathy Johnson. Reproduced courtesy of the Kansas City, Missouri, Board of Parks and Recreation Commissioners.

2-13. A number of techniques can be used to convey shading with line. (a) A pen dragged quickly over the surface of your paper will produce open lines that appear light-struck. (b) Repeated lines can also express shading. Depth of shadow will depend on how closely the lines are spaced. (c) Cross hatching is the traditional method used to express mass and volume in pen-and-ink. (d) Short, choppy lines and dots communicate tone in a freer way. Look at some of Vincent van Gogh's ink drawings for examples of how this technique may be used. (e) Carefully placed stipples are often used to express roundness in scientific illustrations.

Ink makes a very definite black line, without the subtlety so easy to achieve in pencil just by varying pressure on the lead. To achieve a sense of halftone or grays in pen-and-ink, you may need to resort to a number of techniques (Fig. 2-13). The simplest is to drag your nib quickly over the paper's surface, making a broken line that can read as a light-struck

2-12. A round-nibbed pen was used in the Inuit or Eskimo style to loosen up and explore a different way of seeing.

halftone. Repeated lines give the illusion of shading, and their spacing (close or far apart) affects the way the eye reads the gray tones. Classical artists of Europe used cross-hatching to express shades, as did the masters of etching of the nineteenth and early twentieth centuries. Look at a Currier and Ives etching to see how cross-hatching was used to give definition and shape to forms. Repeated lines and cross-hatching are often used to follow the form being described to give roundness to the subject. Look at the ink (and pencil) drawings of Rubens, Botticelli, da Vinci, and Rembrandt to learn how simple repeated lines can be used to express volume.

Short, choppy pen strokes or repeated dots can also be used to add subtlety and value to a line drawing. Vincent van Gogh was a master of the repeated stroke and dot technique. His line work mirrors his later paintings in the way that short strokes were used to follow a form, setting one plane off from another.

Scientific illustrators often use stippling, or repeated dots, to express roundness. Depending on how closely you place the dots,

the apparent lightness or darkness of the form will be seen as shadow by your eye. Look closely at a photograph in a newspaper, using a hand lens if necessary. Here are dots used to convey all tones and shading. That would be much too mechanical for an artist to reproduce, of course, but many people use technical pens to achieve a beautiful subtlety in their work by modifying this principle, as Figure 2-14 demonstrates.

You may also produce subtle grays simply by diluting your ink, but be advised that it makes reproduction more difficult. You can also experiment with applying ink with a small brush instead of a pen. Charles W. Schwartz uses this method in a masterly way, and he prefers the fine detail he is able to achieve (Fig. 2-15). Ink *is* hard on brushes, however, so be sure to wash your brush thoroughly when through. Do not use your favorite watercolor brush in india ink.

Ink drawings are not as malleable as pencil ones. They are not as easy to change and adjust, and unless you put in a long session with an ink eraser, you will accomplish little in erasing an ink

2-14. Blaine Billman, an Idaho artist, carries the dot or pointillist technique to the sublime, often spending 500 or more hours on his sensitive and beautiful pieces. *Alaskan Airways*, by Blaine Billman, © 1982. Reproduced courtesy of the artist.

2-15. A fine brush was used instead of the usual pen to create this ink drawing. *Cottontail Rabbit*, by Charles W. Schwartz. Reproduced courtesy of the artist and the Conservation Commission of the State of Missouri.

drawing. An eraser is used on ink primarily to remove preliminary pencil under-drawing, since too much rubbing with a coarse eraser will abrade the paper. Artists who work for photo reproduction fix little mistakes on ink drawings with retouch white, available at art-supply stores. But since I like my drawings to appear unaltered, I use an electric eraser with a soft pink nib. By using my eraser shield, I can salvage most mistakes without having to redraw the whole piece.

Painting

Oil and acrylic techniques are beyond the scope of this book, although the works of artists who use these media have been included throughout as examples of rendering. Their use is covered in depth in many excellent publications, some of which are listed in the Bibliography. Techniques are specialized, as are the order of seeing and working. In drawing and in watercolor painting, the artist most often works from light to dark, carefully preserving the lightest areas of the composition

A.

B.

Tryst Falls — vertical makes it dramatic, horizontal makes it pastoral & serene.

2-16. Notice the contrasting moods expressed in these two sketches of the same subject in different formats: (a) is dramatic, while (b) is peaceful. Format sketches, by Cathy Johnson. Reproduced courtesy of *The Artist's Magazine*.

from start to finish. With oils, acrylics, and other opaque and semi-opaque media such as gouache, egg tempera, and the newer alkyd paints, the order of seeing, and therefore of working, is usually reversed: the lightest, smallest highlight is often the *last* item of business.

Watercolor painting is covered in detail in chapter 3.

Composition

Consciously or unconsciously, composition is one of the first things we notice about a work of art. We may not call it by that name, but we are aware of a certain flow, a rhythm, a guiding of our eyes into the picture or a focusing of our attention on the center of interest. This is the work of composition in a painting or drawing. Classical artists used what is known as the "golden third," a rule whereby the center of interest is placed one-third of the distance from one side of the painting and one-third up from the bottom or down from the top.

Look at works of art and see if you can find the golden-third principle at work. Use it in your own work to create better compositions and avoid common mistakes. A child's drawing may have a person smack in the center of the page, or the horizon cutting the picture plane in half horizontally; you may make these same "mistakes" if you are not aware. A series of diagonal lines or a single, sweeping, sinuous one will lead the eye into the picture plane more simply than a stark upright or flat horizontal, often with more pleasing results.

It is often said that the center of interest should be well positioned on a page—that is, not radically off to one side, seeming ready to fall off into an abyss. Moreover, it is suggested that a person—or animal—should look into the mass of the picture area instead of at something beyond the edge of the picture. Be *aware* of these rules, practice them, use them, make them a part of your artistic vocabulary—and then, if they do not work to express what you

want in a specific instance, forget them. Consciously breaking a rule to achieve an effect can produce a dramatic, dynamic composition. I like an asymmetrical work, with the subject off-balance at the edge of a large open space. It gives me the *feeling* of space, of distance. If you work consciously, a subject looking away off the edge of the page gives a certain tension, an exciting expectancy. It involves the viewer in an unexpected way. I get a certain pleasure in breaking a compositional rule and breaking it successfully. If my work elicits a response, strikes a chord, makes someone say, "Yes, that's how it really *is*," then I am satisfied.

Format

Format is an important consideration when you are planning a composition. Some subjects lend themselves to a horizontal format, some to a vertical. Subjects such as a broad expanse of open water, a wide prairie, a muddy river—or the 80-inch wingspan of a bald

"NORMAL"

STORMY

SNOWY

establishing mood with values

2-17. These three sketches highlight the strong value patterns to look for in a composition or subject. If your subject has no discernible inherent value pattern, you may want to try a series of quick sketches like these to establish your own. Reproduced courtesy of *The Artist's Magazine*.

bug's-eye view might also be likely candidates for a vertical format; or use the vertical to focus on a portion of a larger landscape. Perhaps a wide vista contains an interesting stratification of fields and hills. By using the vertical format—even an extreme vertical —you can play up the stratification to form interesting, almost abstract patterns.

Format can help you to express mood, as Figure 2-16 shows. When choosing your format, think first how your subject makes you feel. The traditional horizontal format is obviously not the only choice, despite the odd fact that most framers will automatically put the hanger in that direction unless told otherwise.

A Four-Value System

In color theory, values are the degrees of light and dark in the visible world. Our eyes see an incredible range of values, from the whitest white of sunlit snow, blinding in its brilliance, to the delicate pearlescent grays of clouds, through the subtle shades of wet mud at a creek's edge to the bottomless black of a mule deer's eye. The variety of shades can be confusing when we try to draw them, making a jumbled pattern. Any work of art needs a strong value *pattern* (Fig. 2-17) even if the overall work is quite high key (light) or low key (dark). The value pattern is what helps the eye differentiate objects (Fig. 2-18). Light (or the effect of light) is what gives the eye—and the brain—the ability to see things separately.

Think of the hour just before dawn, when everything is gray—

eagle—lend themselves to a horizontal format. Generally speaking, the horizontal format gives a pastoral, peaceful, wide-open-spaces feeling to your work. But a prairie storm might also be well expressed with this format, and it is *not* a peaceful subject, as you know if you have ever witnessed one of the more violent ones up close. Most often the horizontal is used to encompass a broad expanse of landscape, but it is also useful on a more intimate scale.

The vertical format is more dramatic, well suited to a painting of a waterfall or a brilliant bolt of lightning. A tall flower, a slender giraffe, a painting done from a

2-18. The artist has used a very low-key value pattern to express bare trees on a winter day very effectively. The shadows help the tree trunks and patchy snow to stand out in a pattern as complex and interesting as a winter forest. *Winter Woods*, by Keith Hammer. Reproduced courtesy of the artist.

gray hills, gray trees, gray houses. Without light, everything is flat, like shapes cut out of the same gray paper and pasted in a monotone collage. Light gives us the ability to *see*.

One of the most important effects of light is the casting of shadows. Learn to use shadows as value patterns in your work to define negative shapes, to show roundness as a tree turns away from the light, to provide interesting patterns, to explain planes. Look for the darkest darks, the mid-tones, and varied lights; shadows tell you if the ground falls away from an object, undulates softly, or rises sharply behind it. Shadows hold and reflect light—notice how the shadowed edge of a cloud will reflect the

warmth of a wheat field or the cool depth of the ocean. Shadows help define forms. We think of a shadowy world as gloomy and somehow undesirable, but without shadows there would be only the flat, uninteresting glare of two-dimensional shapes. Values found in shadows help us project the truths our eyes can see onto our paper, making our work believable.

Unless you can masterfully convey value, you will probably need to simplify our wonderfully complex world of lights and darks. I use a four-value system in my sketches and drawings to make my work easier to ''read.'' The white of my paper acts as my lightest value, and black is my darkest dark. (In doing water-

colors I seldom use this deepest of values except for small accents. I can mix a variety of grays, from the lightest to the deepest, with ultramarine blue and burnt sienna or umber.) For the purpose of a preliminary sketch, I use this ''black'' as my deepest dark. A light and a dark gray act as my intermediate values. These two represent all the middle tones, and whereas they may vary somewhat in intensity when the sketch is translated to color, the original value pattern will still be evident, giving my work cohesiveness and making sense of planes and shapes.

Train your eye to judge how dark a color is, or use a gray scale next to your color. Squint your eyes a bit to help differentiate the

Format Studies (thumbnail sketches)

LOW Key value study   HIGH Key value study

2-19. Values as well as format were experimented with in these thumbnail sketches. Reproduced courtesy of *The Artist's Magazine*.

values in what you see before you. This simplifies shapes and values and reduces the impact of complicating and confusing colors on the retina. A piece of tinted glass or dark sunglasses also make value patterns easier to see.

You are not obligated to draw the value pattern you *see*, however. If you have passed by on another day, in another season, when cumulus clouds were casting wonderful shadows over the hills or the raking shadows of oncoming evening made dramatic

patterns in the woods, think back to what made the scene memorable to you. Play around with the values in thumbnail drawings in your sketchbook (Fig. 2-19). Try a very high key interpretation of the scene, such as you might see on a snowy January day, or make the time that dramatic moment before the storm finally breaks.

Mood

Mood or ambience may be expressed with the variables of

value. The mood may be light and sun-filled—a June afternoon—or it may be dramatic and thunderous, as when a storm advances across a broad valley. Look for those touches that convey the essence of this mood: the sparkle of light on a calm lake dotted with lily pads and arrowhead plants; dew-bejeweled wings of a dragonfly at dawn; the almost palpably peaceful mood of a mother doe suckling her fawn at dusk. Think of a prairie storm, a snowy winter's day, a mist-filled evening, and consider ways you might express that special ambience in your drawing or painting. These things touch the viewer and tell a story.

Distance, Depth, and the Effects of Light

Earth's atmosphere—our air—gives the feeling of distance that our eyes perceive; it suggests effects we can use in our work as well. Water, particles of dust, pollutants, all are suspended in air and are visible from a distance, although they are invisible in our immediate vicinity. On a day of high humidity, even the nearest hills look as if they wear a gauze of pale blue, and the farther hills may almost disappear into the blue of the sky. The dust suspended in the lower atmosphere gives a sunset its vermilion glow, and water particles in the sky may reflect light back to us as rainbows or sun dogs, those short, vertical bursts of prismatic color on either side of the sun, visible most often in winter. They occur when the sun's rays shine through a light cloud cover, touching off a burst of color in the same way a rainbow forms by the action of light on water droplets when it rains. See chapter 7, on the landscape, for further information about capturing the feeling of atmosphere and distance.

Using Negative Space

In your drawing, the shape of the object itself is the positive space or positive shape. As in a photographic negative, the areas that surround the positive shape define and explain it. They can become an integral part of your design. You can use negative space in a very *positive* way.

In her book *Drawing on the Right Side of the Brain*, Betty Edwards suggests drawing the negative shapes when the positive ones have become too symbolically

2-20. Negative shapes were used to define the positive shape of the cat in this pencil drawing. I find pets to be invaluable and handy models, and drawing them provides the fundamentals for drawing more elusive wildlife. *Westport*, by Cathy Johnson.

embedded in our mind's eye for us to see them clearly. For instance, you may see an eye as an elongated and pointed oval with a circle in the middle, symbolically, which is all well and good if your subject is facing you directly—symbolically speaking, an eye might very well be drawn that way. But when the subject faces away in a three-quarter or side view, the eye's shape changes dramatically and can no longer be drawn accurately from the shape preprogrammed in our mind. In order to banish the preconceived form and draw the eye accurately Edwards suggests drawing not the positive object, the eye, but the negative shape surrounding it. Try this when drawing a complicated detail such as the ear or nose of an animal, where subtle turnings and inner shapes might be confusing. Do not look at the object but at the

area adjacent to it, and draw that.

Negative-space drawings can produce some very interesting effects. Oil painters and others who use opaque mediums often use this, consciously or otherwise, when they "punch holes" in a tree canopy with sky color—they are not painting the tree but describing the not-tree (thereby making a quite believable tree). I have used this technique in Figure 2-20. Rather than trying to express my cream-colored cat's pale shape by drawing it alone and isolated, I used the dark design behind her to show where she began and the background ended. In that way, almost as a bonus, I was not tempted into an overworked rendering of fur and other details.

Complicated patterns, such as interlaced branches, might well be expressed by first drawing the negative shapes that surround them. Then if you wish, you may

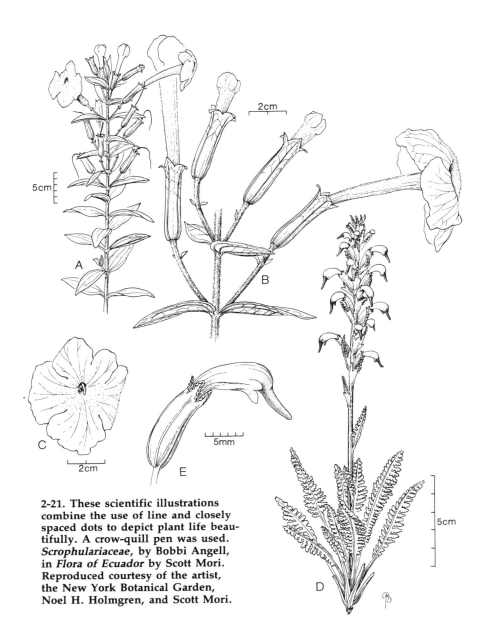

2-21. These scientific illustrations combine the use of line and closely spaced dots to depict plant life beautifully. A crow-quill pen was used. *Scrophulariaceae*, by Bobbi Angell, in *Flora of Ecuador* by Scott Mori. Reproduced courtesy of the artist, the New York Botanical Garden, Noel H. Holmgren, and Scott Mori.

go back and add all the detail you like in the positive shapes, always maintaining a balance between the positive and negative.

Using Line to Express Life

Often, a beautifully pure line drawing will be the most satisfying way to draw what we see before us. Scientific illustrators often use only line for diagnostic drawings (Fig. 2-21) to avoid distracting patterns created by shadows. Look at the drawings in Peterson's *A Field Guide to Wildflowers*

or *Simon and Schuster's Guide to Trees* to see some first-rate botanical line drawings. These delicate lines perfectly capture the intricate detail of flower, tree, leaf, and seed.

A lively linear quality is evident in many drawings when the lines are allowed to vary in weight and thickness (Fig. 2-22). As discussed earlier in the section on pencil drawing, heavier lines may be used to show things that are close to you, lighter ones to indicate distance. The eye perceives more detail up close than it does farther

away—the leaf that is near you is visible in all its perfection and imperfection; small insect chewings, intricate interweaving of the webs of veins carrying nutrients to the leaf and to the tree itself. The leaf on a tree on the far hill blends into the mass of leaves in the tree's canopy and can only be expressed symbolically or through a continuous tone broken by shadow areas. Use that natural phenomenon in your work to express life through the use of line. Use detail to bring things closer to the viewer and simplify objects in the distance.

Frederick Franck is a master of the use of line to express life. In his books (see Bibliography), he uses delicate, weblike lines in an almost seismographic way, as he says, to trace the life he sees before him.

Color

Color is one of the most exciting tools an artist can use to render life. It can also be the most dangerous in the sense that it can distract if used without a solid grounding, a good reason. Color has fascinated artists for centuries, and basic color theory is an important tool in understanding how to use color.

I am assuming that you are familiar with the basics: hue, value, intensity, and the use of a color wheel. You will have experimented with color schemes and used the various effects in your work. A complex subject like color theory is beyond the scope of this book—it merits a volume of its own. For the reader who wants to learn more, several books are listed in the Bibliography.

Nature is often profligate with color, ignoring all man-made rules and theoretical color schemes. Nature's palette contains all the hues of the rainbow. Why does that not look confusing, brassy, overdone? Perhaps because the bright colors—of flowers, butterflies,

2-22. A very lively line was used here to capture these sheep with charcoal pencil in a loose, free rendering. *Suffolk Sheep*, by Sharon Stolzenberger. Reproduced courtesy of the artist.

birds—generally appear in small, precious doses. The overall scheme may be blue and green with only bright accents, of yellow sunflowers and purple ironweed. Take a lesson from nature and use your brightest brights as small accents. Even in painting a rainbow, with its stained-glass primaries and prismatic gradations, note the effects of atmosphere and distance. The colors appear slightly muted or paled, and the rainbow itself is but a small part of the overall landscape. ''Many people make the mistake of painting a rainbow as if it were a decal in the back window of someone's car,'' artist Jim Hamil says. ''Notice, the next time you see a rainbow, how subdued it actually is, however bright it may appear in contrast to dark clouds.'' To prove this to yourself, hold up something dyed red the next time you see a rainbow, so the red object seems to float in the sky next to it. The rainbow's red is delicate, pure, transparent in comparison.

Perhaps the best thing we can do in using color in our work is to really look at what we are painting and to depict what is there. Pigment as it comes straight from the tube may sometimes need to be modified with a touch of red or blue, warmed or cooled slightly.

Make no mistake—nature *is* full of color. By learning to see what is inherent in that color and accentuating it, we make our paintings believable. We can use color symbolically to elicit that same response of ''Yes, that's how it really is.'' Where color is reflected back into a shadow, where clouds pick up the warmth of July's wheat fields, where back-lit trees seem to glow from within with October fire—*see* what is there and find a way to express it. A touch of subtle color is usually enough, however, unless you are painting the setting sun's rays on the Grand Canyon or the carnival colors of a flower garden. Remember the subtle shades of nature: the deep refractive blues of a snowbank as it faces away from the light, glacial and icy; the rich, ruddy tones hiding in the heartwood of a walnut tree; the glowing whites of a bloodroot flower in early spring.

An artist friend of mine has said that color is the most exciting thing in the world to her and simply remembering the light glinting off a stand of golden aspens was enough to set her heart racing and her hand itching for a paintbrush. Color can express that excitement.

CHAPTER THREE

Watercolor Tips

3-1

Watercolor is my medium, my frustration and my joy. It seems to me to be the most natural choice for expressing the freshness and excitement of nature because it is itself fresh and exciting. Watercolor is freedom and discipline, pleasure and pain. No one can tell you how to paint in watercolor—the medium is too changeable for that. With watercolor, you will learn each day you paint; the medium itself teaches, through what watercolorists have called "happy accidents." The exact same thing will never happen twice in just the same way. However, you can learn to use those happy accidents to add a certain piquancy to your work.

In painting nature, we need a way to depict the way that light affects what we see—we need ways to render flowing water (Fig. 3-2),

soft fur, bottomless depths, the craggy roughness of a cliff's face. We need ways to paint the hunter's moon rising like a bubble in the night sky. I will try to share with you a few of the things I have learned to convey this magic using watercolor. You will find your own ways, discover your own tricks that will make your work truly yours.

Palettes

A number of different kinds of watercolor palettes are available, ranging from the clean expanse of an enameled butcher tray to the deep-welled palette of luncheon-plate size that is used by many painters of miniatures. You alone will know which palette will best suit your needs. Do you like to paint small, meticulous, careful

studies? A small, deep-welled palette or a portable metal watercolor box might be just the ticket (Fig. 3-3). Do you like to mix juicy, profligate washes with a huge brush for free, fresh flow? The butcher's tray or other large palette is what you will need to allow room to dip that big brush into the mounds of paint and mix those big washes. If you do large renderings, you will want a big palette. Rex Brandt uses a round plastic palette with color arranged around the outside rim like a rainbow and produces some wonderfully fresh paintings with this setup, but I need more mixing room to create palette grays (those everything-but-the-kitchen-sink grays that come from mixing whatever happens to be on my mixing surface at the time) and still have room for a clean wash.

3-2. This watercolor imparts a real feeling of the flow of the river on a cloudy day. *Fishing on the Blue River*, © 1975 by Jim Hamil, in *Farmland* by Harold Hamil. Reproduced courtesy of the artist and Farmland Industries.

3-3. A tiny palette with deep wells was used to paint this exquisite botanical study. *Violas*, by Eleanor Lewis. Reproduced courtesy of the artist.

Some people even keep two large palettes going at one time to make sure at least one is relatively clean. I have used my John Pike palette for ten years and enjoy the large mixing area and pigment wells with dams to keep colors unsullied. It has a lid that doubles as extra mixing space when needed.

Since watercolor is a transparent medium, you will need a white surface for mixing colors, to help you see how they will look on the white of your paper. An aluminum pie plate spray-painted white will work just as well as an expensive palette.

A good artist's or professional grade of pigments is your best investment. The discount-store kind—or even the student grade of some of the better brands—will fade or flake off with time. Even some of the finest brand-name pigments are fugitive, meaning they will fade in moderate light conditions, but manufacturers of good watercolor pigments offer color charts that let you know beforehand which colors are fugitive. If you are working for reproduction, not posterity, you may want to use that special fugitive color, but I usually prefer to stay on the side of permanence if at all possible. A painting I did some years ago still hangs in my bank, where I wince each time I see how my spring-green grass has turned chartreuse. If you want to save on pigments, you can paint with a limited palette—orange, violet, or green is easy enough to mix yourself if the budget is tight.

Unlike the visually pure colors of the spectrum, available pigments do not mix to form such wonderfully pure secondary and tertiary colors. In order to resolve this difficulty, I use a warm and a cool version of each of my primaries. For instance, thalo blue is considered a cool blue, touched with green, so it mixes well with yellow to make a good, clear green. Ultramarine blue, on the other hand, is a warm blue with a hint of red in it, so while it makes a fine purple, the green it produces is a little weak and muddy. My own palette consists of these two blues, alizarin crimson (cool) and cadmium red (warm), cadmium yellow medium (warm) and lemon yellow (cool), plus the indispensable earth tones. I like burnt umber, burnt sienna, and raw sienna for most things: raw sienna generally takes the place of yellow ochre for me. Cobalt blue is usually added to my repertoire, as is manganese blue, Hooker's green deep, and sepia umber. Most of these extras can be mixed satisfactorily using the primaries and earth colors, though, so I could do without them if I were a bit less lazy. I make rich, luminous darks by mixing ultramarine blue with burnt umber or burnt sienna, thalo green and alizarin crimson, or thalo blue and burnt sienna.

Always arrange your palette in the same way—that is, lay out your colors in the same order—to save yourself from wasting precious time looking in an unfamiliar place for that necessary blue as your wash dries beyond the optimum time to add fresh color. (Keep a plastic spray bottle nearby filled with clean water to spritz your painting to retard too-rapid drying if necessary—although this, too, must be done at the right time or you will have pale dots where the water hits). Some artists prefer to arrange colors prismatically, others keep lights and darks separated. It does not really matter how you lay out your pigments—whatever seems most comfortable to you is the best way to do it.

Preparation

It helps to set up your studio or painting area in a familiar pattern as well. Keep your coffee cup well away from your paint water, or you will inevitably end up with a Maxwell House wash. How you set up depends on whether you are right- or left-handed, whether you like to paint sitting down or standing up or a combination of the two, how much room you have, where your primary light source is—any number of factors can influence your arrangement. But if you set up in a consistent manner, then no matter where you paint (at home, in a class, in the field), the frustrations caused by searching for equipment can be kept to a minimum. I like my palette on my right, with the blues closest to me and reds and yellows at the top to keep them relatively unsullied by drips. My water jar (or jars—sometimes I use two, one full of clean water for fresh washes) is just above the palette, and my jar of brushes is just above that. I painted for years on a slanted drafting board until I decided I preferred the additional control of a flat wash. You can always tilt your board at the strategic moment to control pigment flow or prop it up if you want.

A synthetic sponge is near or on my palette to soak up excess pigment in my brush, and a box of tissues is within easy reach for mistakes or adjustments. I keep a plastic spray bottle with clean water hung by its trigger handle from the open drawer of my taboret and additional tools and gadgets on my right, so they are always near.

Some people insist that you *must* stretch watercolor paper that is lighter in weight than 300 pounds, to which I say hogwash. Stretching paper the traditional way, by soaking it, taping it to a board, and allowing it to dry thoroughly *will* give you a smooth, wrinkle-free surface to work on, and if you are using a light paper (70-pound) for watercolor, such preparation is necessary. But I learned years ago that

3-4. A variety of effects can be achieved with a flat lettering brush on smooth paper.

FLAT (LETTERING) BRUSH (smooth, hot press paper)

dry 140-pound paper taped with 1 ½-inch-wide masking tape to a smooth Masonite board will behave quite nicely, and save you the time spent in paper preparation. Tape down your paper and you can begin to work immediately. The minimal buckling that occurs will almost always flatten back out as the painting dries. When the painting is thoroughly dry, carefully pull away the masking tape, and you are left with nice clean edges that you can either incorporate into the design or cover with the mat before framing. These clean edges often help me to judge if a painting is finished, rather like using a trial mat; if I need to work further, I simply retape.

Simple Exercises

If you have never painted with watercolor before, take a bit of time to familiarize yourself with some of the techniques.

Get to know your brushes. You will probably have bought a couple of round, pointed watercolor brushes of varying sizes and a flat or two. Try them out on some inexpensive paper. In fact, whenever I get a new brush I put it through a few test runs to see what I can expect. Play with your brushes, turning them this way and that. Use old brushes or cheap ones to try some of the rougher effects of scumbling or scrubbing, using choppy, quick strokes or lifting paint with clear water, literally scrubbing it off your paper's surface. Turn flats to try out the edge or the tip as well as the broad side of the brush. Turn them as you paint to create wonderful thick-and-thin lines, for painting grasses, leaves, tree branches, crane's legs. We all hope to find the perfect brush someday, the brush that will do just what we want it to, every time—the brush that will erase our frustrations and make us all Michelangelos—but it will never happen. Getting to know and use the ones we have is a creditable second best, however, so practice all the possible strokes for a while, and try them out on different papers as well. Use your brush to dot or stamp, to make light graceful swirls, or wiggle it back and forth to make wavy lines. This is the kind of play that will stand you in good stead later when you wonder how to capture that particularly graceful sway of cattail leaves in a light breeze—just remember those long, sweeping strokes using your whole arm, and you will be on your way. With this practice you will have developed that special confidence that comes from knowing your equipment and what it will do. Figures 3-4, 3-5, 3-6, and 3-7 show only a few of the possible brushstrokes you may find interesting or useful when painting from nature.

A "wash" is the application of watercolor pigment—and enough water to dilute it to the desired tone—to your paper; there are

SEVERAL SIZES OF ROUND WATERCOLOR BRUSHES (smooth, hot press paper)

3-5. These are a few of the effects possible with a round brush on smooth paper.

round brush on rough paper

flat brush on rough paper

3-6. Compare the effects here of flat and round brushes on rough paper with those made with the same brushes on smooth paper in Figures 3-4 and 3-5.

3-7. Specialty brushes and tools, including fan brushes, rigger brushes, palette knives, bamboo pens, and natural sponges, can be used in different ways to achieve a number of effects. Think of ways you might use these tools in depicting nature, and experiment on your own.

3-8. Consider the varied strokes the artist used in this watercolor to express the essence of nature, not simply what he saw before him. His unique vision shines like the sun. *Drought Mirage*, by Charles Burchfield. Reproduced by permission of the Nelson-Atkins Museum of Art, Kansas City, Missouri (Nelson Fund), gift of Mr. and Mrs. Morton I. Sosland.

a.

flat wash (well, reasonably flat)

b.

graded wash

c.

brush dragged lightly over paper surface

d.

pigment dropped into wet wash

3-9. (a) Watercolor washes can be created and modified for different effects. A flat wash is one of the most basic in watercolor. A bead of color is carried down the page with a fully loaded brush. Slant your paper slightly for best results. (b) A graded wash executed just like a flat wash, except that the brush is dipped in water, rather than pigment, for each successive stroke. (c) Dragging the brush lightly over the paper's surface allows the paper to sparkle through your brushstrokes. This effect is useful in depicting broken shadows, sunlight on water, leaf canopies—consider the possibilities. (d) Pigment dropped into a wet wash creates bright explosions of color.

several types used to achieve various effects. A *flat wash*, for example, is just what it seems: a smooth application of color, unvarying in hue or value. A *graded wash* goes from a strong saturation of pigment to a pale, diluted tone—or vice-versa. Learning to make a few simple washes is like learning your ABCs—you cannot "write" a good watercolor without them. After you master the basics, you can devise your own particular techniques, and that is the most satisfying part of all—

learning to express what you see with your own special vision. Vincent van Gogh did not see like Rembrandt, Edward Hopper did not see like Charles Burchfield (Fig. 3-8), and your own vision is unique and valid as well.

A flat wash (Fig. 3-9a) is really the easiest of all—just be sure to mix enough pigment to see you through the entire wash evenly, since it is almost impossible to mix an identical color. With your paper slightly tilted, make a smooth stroke across the top of the wash

area. A rounded bead of color will appear on the lower edge of the stroke: when you make the next stroke, you simply pick up this bead and carry it with each successive stroke to the end of the wash. If need be, go back and pick up the last bead with a damp (not dripping) brush or with a piece of tissue, or it will bleed back into your lovely smooth wash as it dries.

A graded wash (Fig. 3-9b) is just a flat wash with clear water rather than pigment added to each brushstroke to lighten it. Make your first stroke (or two, or three, depending on how far into the picture plane you want your color full strength) pure wash, then with each new stroke dip your brush into clean water. The wash will flow down the tilted paper, fading with each dilution. You can carry this as far as you want or until you run out of paper—it is even possible to work back the other way and add more and more pigment till you have a good strong color at the bottom as well. You can introduce other colors instead of clear water to make interesting gradations of color, or allow successive graded washes to dry thoroughly before adding another on top, grading in the other direction (Fig. 3-10).

Now branch out a bit and drag your brush lightly across the paper's surface (Fig. 3-9c). Hold the brush nearly horizontal to the paper's surface so only the high points of the paper will pick up the color. This technique is useful in painting the broken texture of rotted wood, sunlight sparkling on a lake, cirrus clouds scooting high across an otherwise clear sky—look at what you have done and think how you might use that effect in your work.

Make another wash of a light pigment and drop stronger colors into it—they will explode into the wet wash or flow in unexpected ways (Fig. 3-9d). This can produce some exciting effects. I like to drop wet pigment into a wash where sunlight strikes a leaf or where a bird's glossy feathers reflect the blue of the sky. The colors bounced back into a shadow area are easily depicted by dropping a subtle hint of the subject's local color (true color unaffected by light or shade) back into the coolness of the shadows. Today as I walked in the woods a column of sunlight broke through to light up golden buckeye leaves in the understory and strike fire from the ground in the form of warm lights on the dead leaves. The warmth was reflected back onto the underside of a fallen, rotting log, giving the shadowed area a burnt sienna glow—that is just how I would try to capture that moment in time.

You may wish to try out *wet-in-wet* effects; some artists find they are more able to produce a smooth wash, flat or graded, if the paper surface is first wetted with clear water. You may even wish to soak your paper thoroughly and place it on a nonabsorbent surface (glass, plastic, formica) to keep it from drying as you work. Keep it wet until you are satisfied.

Wet-in-wet painting is more difficult to control than painting done directly onto dry paper, but it is often exciting and spontaneous. Soft, diaphanous shapes often occur when you are painting wet-in-wet. It is nearly impossible to paint fine, sharp details while your paper still has its slick, wet shine, but if you wait until the surface dries, you can achieve a wide variety of effects, from soft- to hard-edged.

Glazing is a more controlled watercolor technique, and one often used by the English school of painters in the late nineteenth century. Instead of painting wet-into-wet or any of the other somewhat splashy—and tricky—techniques, in glazing you simply add successive washes as each dries thoroughly. Subsequent layers are

3-10. Graded washes artfully express the petals and leaves of peonies. *Peonies*, by Peggy McKeehan. Reproduced courtesy of the artist.

applied quickly and lightly so as not to lift the underwashes. Great detail and depth are possible with this method, and colors tend to stay fresher than if the same number of pigments were introduced into a wet wash, where they would mix into mud.

Dry-Brush Technique

This technique is related to the dragging exercise discussed above, but in that case your brush was in fact quite full of wet pigment; the way you manipulated it, nearly flat on the paper, produced the broken, dry-brush *effect*. In the *technique* called dry brush, you may be using almost straight pigment, virtually undiluted by water, or a pale mixture in a brush wiped dry on a damp sponge or tissue. You can get great detail and texture using dry brush. The drawing in Figure 3-1 is a combination of wet-in-wet un-

derwash (wet paper, wet wash) and a dry-brush application on top when the paper was thoroughly dry.

Albrecht Durer was a master of the dry-brush technique, as many of his more famous works attest. *The Young Hare* is amazingly detailed without being overworked and seems to capture the essence of the gangly adolescent (Fig. 3-11). Andrew Wyeth is a contemporary master of dry brush. Look at some of his studies for larger works to gain insight into how what *can* be a rather stiff technique in the wrong hands can be combined with freely painted washes for an exciting result. (Look at, be inspired by, but do not copy—there is only one Wyeth, and there is only one you. There are all too many poor-man's Wyeths—or Andy Warhols for that matter—around now.)

That is not to say, incidentally, that the tradition of imitating the

masters is not instructive and worthwhile when you are learning to draw. But your personal vision will be just as exciting if you let it free, and certainly much more satisfying to you in the long run than trying to reproduce someone else's.

Painting in Sequence

It is generally best to do a watercolor in sequence, working specifically from light to dark (Fig. 3-12). I generally begin with a light pencil sketch directly on my watercolor paper. The lighter washes help set the pencil lines and give a feeling of where the painting is going. The first wash need not be pale or pastel, but you *will* want to retain your lightest lights at this stage, as well as the sparkle of pure white paper for highlights. They can be recaptured later but often at the expense of freshness.

After the first wash is completely dry (and it may cover the entire paper with a number of hues, rather than covering one section or being one color only), proceed with your middle values, building tones and beginning to develop depth.

I like to add a bit of dark as I lay in the middle values, to give myself something to compare later washes against, just to get a feeling of how dark I plan to go, but proceed with caution if you do this. Darks may lift up in subsequent washes and lose their clean edges or dissolve into fuzzy, muddy messes.

Unless you are adding fine detail at this intermediate, middle-value stage, it is often best to spray areas with clear water before working back into them. Do not wet and rework areas until they are thoroughly dry. You can create soft edges by painting into this newly moistened area, while avoiding hard edges you might get by adding a wet wash into a drying area.

Your darkest or brightest colors come last. Used sparingly, they will add sparkle to your painting. A long time ago I learned an interesting phenomenon: if an area has gotten muddy or looks too dark, add a small, even darker dark within it or nearby. That will make your muddy area appear lighter and cleaner.

Ted Kautzky was one of the few watercolorists to successfully flout the light-to-dark rule, but he had terrific control and painted rather dry. With wet-in-wet techniques, painting dark to light produces a mud puddle in short order.

Another watercolor sequence, shared with most other forms of art, is starting big and working small. That is, use your biggest brush to paint the broadest areas first, then graduate to smaller brushes and finer detail. You may not need to paint anywhere near as much detail as you had originally planned if you develop a habit of stopping once in a while to look at your work. If it looks finished—or almost so—stop. If you are not sure, stop anyway—you can always go back later when you have had a chance to mull it over awhile. I often tighten down on only a few areas with intricate detail and let others stay fresh and washy. Figure 3-13 shows how artist Laney Hicks effectively uses this technique. I like the tension and excitement this produces: it involves the viewer's emotions more than a painting that is spelled out with too much detail; it allows him to finish with his own imagination, invest it with his own creativity. I have the greatest admiration for artists who do work habitually with great detail, but I cannot imagine doing it. I would lose the spark, the joy—and an elusive sense of conversation with the viewer.

Tricks of the Trade

Watercolor may sound quite tricky enough to the uninitiated, but take my word for it, these tricks, shown in Figure 3-14, are fun and very effective. They get the job done without overworking an area.

Not all tricks can—or even should—be used in one painting, or course, but used judiciously, a few well-chosen and compatible tricks will give your work an energy that is difficult to attain with straight painting techniques.

First Wash - biggest brushes, lightest values

Second Wash — Middle tones

3-12. This demonstration shows the traditional method of painting in sequence from light to dark in watercolor. It also shows the progression from large simple shapes to more sharply defined details.

Final Wash or washes — add darks, details, adjust values
Small brush if needed

3-13. The visual trick of tightening down in a few areas focuses the viewer's eye on the center of interest in this beautiful watercolor. *A Pair*, by Laney Hicks. Reproduced courtesy of the artist.

Spatter into wet and dry wash

Clean water spattered into wet wash

table salt into damp wash

table salt into wet wash

liquid mask in damp wash

India ink in wash

liquid mask, dried + painted over

India ink in clear water

3-14. Watercolor tricks, used judiciously, can add excitement and freshness to your work.

3-15. Spatter and scraping were used in this study of a shell.

Spatter is a most useful technique if not overdone (Fig. 3-15). Pick up a fair amount of pigment on a stencil brush, bristle brush, old toothbrush, or what have you, and flick droplets of paint at your work. I like using an old stencil brush best since I can control fairly well where the droplets land when I run my thumb over the edge of the bristles. I can even control direction by the angle of my paper in relation to the brush. Juicier droplets will spatter off a soft, round watercolor brush, with less controllable but still interesting results. This gives a bit of texture to ice or snow, mud or water.

Spatter can also help freshen areas that have gotten a bit overworked. You may either spatter with paint or clear water, into a wet or dry wash (if you use water alone in a dry wash, however, not much will show for your efforts). Mask off with paper areas you want to keep pristine.

Spatter can be used to convey the feeling of a sandy beach, rich humus, the light, lacy leaves of spring, wildflowers sprinkled on a field of grasses. I like to use it to add a bit of texture to leaf masses and weeds, or even to give the effect of melting snow.

Salt is another device that is wonderful if used in moderation. It seems to work best dropped into darker colors, while they are still fairly wet. The salt repels water and leaves a sparkle where it falls. Brush the salt away only when the paint is *thoroughly* dry.

On humid days you may need to supplement drying with a hand-held hair dryer, something I do quite often, whether I am using salt or not.

Salt is useful to depict sparkles on snow or ice, sand on a beach, field flowers, frost on a window. You might want to combine the effects of salt and spatter to give the viewer the feel of an ancient, pockmarked cliff face, sparkling with mica. A mixture of table and kosher salt will add variety. If you want, tip your board as the wash dries to give the salt's action a directional feel.

Masking fluid (frisket) is a latex product that is painted on wet and left to dry before painting over it. Use an old or inexpensive brush, or lather your bristles with soap to enable you to wash it out when finished. Apply with a bamboo pen or palette knife if you prefer. By applying masking fluid in areas where you do not want paint to go, you can retain the whites of tiny flowers, intricate shapes of light-struck limbs, the thin lines of a bird's legs, or an animal silhouetted against a dark forest. Rub it off with your finger or a rubber cement pickup when your painting is completely dry. Use liquid frisket sparingly, as it does leave hard, white edges. You may want to go back in with a brush moistened in clear water to soften

3-16. India ink was drawn into the wet watercolor wash with a crow-quill pen to add unpredictable, lively lines to this quick study of a cliff face.

3-17. These samples show what happens when wet or dry washes are manipulated by scratching, scraping, blotting, or erasing. Lights can be reestablished using these techniques, or the paper can be bruised while the wash is wet to make the fibers accept more pigment. Bruising or scraping the paper can be used to depict light-struck grasses, fine twigs, and other delicate subjects.

wire brush into damp wash

end of brush into damp wash

fingernail, fingerprints

picked up wash with damp natural sponge

dry tissue   damp tissue

scraping, scratching, erasing, masking & washing out in dry wash

3-18. Demuth used a variety of watercolor techniques including graded washes, glazing, and blotting in this still-life study. *Green Pears*, by Charles Demuth (1929). Reproduced by permission of the Yale University Art Gallery: The Philip Goodwin Collection.

those glaring whites, or paint the protected areas with color (Fig. 3-14).

India ink can be used to draw into a wet wash. Lines will explode and flow in an unpredictable way, so watch out! Use it where you are sure you want the excitement of not knowing exactly what will happen. It is useful in painting fissures in a cliff's face, frostkilled weeds, and other irregular lines (Fig. 3-16). Drawing into a clear-water wash will produce more dramatic effects; drawing (or dropping beads of ink) into a darker wash will produce a smoky, subtle effect.

Scratching involves marring, cutting, scraping, or bruising the paper's surface, either before applying a wash, while it is wet, or after the painting has dried (Fig. 3-17). Interesting effects can be achieved by waiting until your wash has lost its wet-wet shine and then scraping the surface with a fingernail, the end of your brush, a curved-blade craft knife, or a wire brush. If done before or during the execution of a painting, while your wash is quite wet, scratching will bruise the paper's fibers, enabling them to absorb more pigment, and creating lines that are darker than your wash. Scratching can effectively give the feel of grass, splitting lines in aging wood, tall weeds, or twigs. I often "fingerpaint," using my fingernail to scrape into a wash for additional texture. Waiting until your wash has lost its shine before scraping will result in *lighter* lines as pigment is pushed out of the way.

Tissue is a ubiquitous aid useful for more than mopping up mistakes or catching a sneeze. Texture can be added to washes by blotting with a dry or damp tissue or paper towel, an effective means of depicting uneven ground textures, rocks, lights on leaf canopies, and bark textures, as well as of lifting paint to create the highlights in light-struck areas on a bird's wing or animal's back (see Fig. 3-17). You can also use a wadded tissue as a tool to apply paint.

Dry-wash manipulation can be employed if a painting has dried and you want to lift out a cloud, a frosty strand of grass, or even a flower shape. Erasers—ink or other types—can be used to pick out soft lights (use the eraser gently to avoid abrading your paper

3-19. The atmospheric quality of dusk is captured in this small watercolor. *Pasture Brook*, by Thomas Aquinas Daly. Reproduced courtesy of the artist.

if you plan to work color back into the area). This technique is useful in locating a rainbow in your already dry sky wash.

To lift out more intricate forms, cut a mask from heavy poster board, stencil material, or vinyl, to protect those areas not to be sponged, and lay it in place on your painting. Hold it firmly, as flat on the paper's surface as possible. With a clean, damp sponge, rub the surface until you achieve the desired degree of lightness (a hard-surfaced watercolor paper or board like Arches or Strathmore will take this somewhat rough handling better than some of the softer-finished papers). Then lift the mask immediately and blot up excess water and pigment that has worked its way under the edge of

the mask. I created the flower shape shown in Figure 3-17 using this technique.

An eraser shield is also useful for erasing more exact forms than is possible freehand. The three small shapes in the sample were done with a shield. You can lift out the mid-rib of a leaf or indicate light illuminating a tree limb with this technique—a patient person could show a branch full of leaves with the sun glinting off them with this method.

Painting with a New "Brush"

Some of my favorite painting tools are not brushes at all. I use an old pointed palette knife to scratch my paper's surface and to paint weeds and twigs. (Remove lac-

quer from a new knife's metal blade by holding it in a flame for a moment or by soaking it in lacquer remover, or the watercolor will bead right off.) A natural sponge is good for painting textures; a wire brush makes interesting texture for grass in a wet wash (see Fig. 3-17). A bamboo pen can be used to draw calligraphic lines; and a broken stick, to paint natural-looking twigs. You may find the perfect "brush" is not a brush at all but a dowel broken to an uneven point. Fingers come in handy too, as do fingernails as mentioned before. Look around you—there are a world of possibilities out there. Whatever you use—a ninety-dollar red sable or your own fingertips—enjoy yourself. Keep that sense of discovery.

CHAPTER FOUR

Small Plants and Flowers

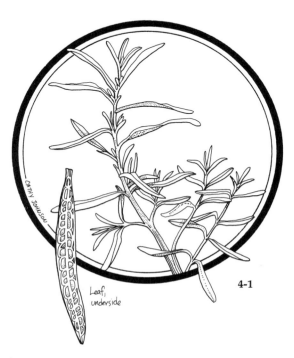

4-1

Most young people find botany a dull study. So it is, as taught from the text-books in the schools: but study it yourself in the fields and woods, and you will find it a source of perennial delight.'' John Burroughs, author and naturalist, wrote these words before the stock-market crash in 1929, before World War II, before television, before Vietnam, or any of the other events that have shaped and shaken our lives. They are still true today. Because this is my favorite field of nature study, I have chosen it as the first subject area to discuss.

All my life I have loved wildflowers, felt delight in coming upon Dutchman's-breeches unexpected in the spring or bicolored, velvety bird's-foot violets in the Missouri Ozarks. I remember the excitement I felt the day I found a jack-in-the-pulpit in the woods and rushed home for my paints and brushes—almost like finding buried treasure. Lying on my stomach in the dead weeds and new spring growth, I painted one of the best things I have ever done, spurred on by the pure joy of discovery. I loved the way the light shone through the ''pulpit'' of delicate green with its elegant maroon stripes and how it reflected off the deeper green leaves.

There is no substitute for careful observation in drawing plants. In a large watercolor I will often symbolize tree shapes, plants, and twigs, but only after grounding myself with firsthand observation. And in a careful study or scientific illustration of a plant, such as Figure 4-2, close examination of the subject is essential.

I am often reminded of high-school biology classes—it is amazing how often memories of pistils and stamens, cambium layers and photosynthesis will bubble back to the surface, sending me off to search for the appropriate field guide to refresh memories or to learn more. One Christmas, my understanding husband presented me with a microscope and a tiny pocket-sized field microscope. With these two instruments and my grandfather's cherished hand lens, I can step inside the life of the plant, entering an almost mystical world of tiny, jewel-like cells, minuscule capillaries bearing nutrients—it is like stepping into a world described by J. R. R. Tolkien. Even if you examine them closely with only the naked eye, you will see that plants and flowers are covered with a network of cells that catch the light, sending back millions of miniature prismatic light-bursts. Our own skin, our hair, and even our fingernails, in fact, share this rainbowlike phenomenon with the plant world.

One way to examine the wonders of the plant world is by studying the images produced by Kirlian photography, a fascinating discipline that is apparently able to capture on film the electrical field of objects.

The science of botany, the world of Tolkien, and the mysteries of Kirlian photography may seem quite removed from rendering plants, but they all offer a means of helping us look beyond, enabling us to shed our preconceived notions of how flowers look, how leaves are made. It is amazing to realize that each flower is constructed as it is especially to fit its niche in the web of nature (Fig. 4-3). A spotted jewelweed invites a pollinating insect inside, a kind of "come into my parlor" design, while a black-eyed Susan lifts its daisylike face to all comers, offering a broad landing strip to bees, butterflies, and other hungry creatures.

To depict plants accurately, it helps to have an idea of the functions the various parts serve. What are their names, their purposes? You may want to do a very detailed field sketch of an unfamiliar plant and then research it further.

4-3. This page from one of my field sketchbooks explores the variety of wildflowers found in a very small area of the park.

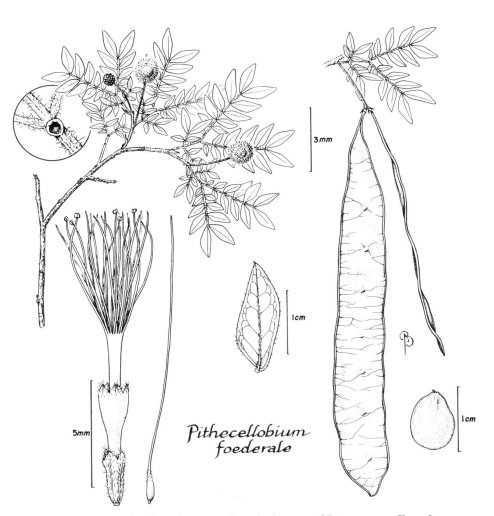

Pithecellobium foederale

4-2. This careful study of a mimosa evokes the beauty of botany as well as the facts. It was drawn from a pressed specimen for the New York Botanical Garden. *Pithecellobium foederale*, by Bobbi Angell. Reproduced courtesy of the artist.

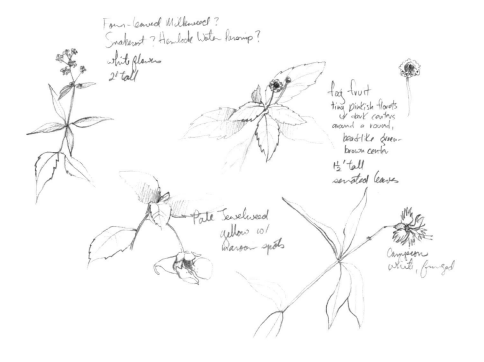

4-4. In these preliminary drawings of milkweed, done as research for illustrating a story in *Sports Afield*, I tried to capture the feel of the plant, and I made careful color notes as well. Notice how the leaf shapes are foreshortened so the leaves seem to come toward the viewer. A bolder line on nearer edges helped reinforce the illusion.

4-5. Notice how the artist has used simplified but accurate forms for the leaf shapes underneath to give believability and depth to this clump of dayflowers. He has also used value to keep these secondary leaf shapes in the background. Detail from *Water's Edge*, by Keith Hammer. Reproduced courtesy of the artist.

It is a common difficulty to fit the three-dimensional form of a plant onto the flat plane of the paper. In order to give the illusion of depth, do not overlook the effects of foreshortening and perspective. Do not draw what you *think* is happening or worry overmuch about getting shapes right; just draw what you *see* and it will look right whether it makes sense to your logical left brain or not. Closer leaves can be rendered with more detail while those that are farther away can be simplified visually (Fig. 4-4). In Figure 4-5, artist Keith Hammer has simplified the shapes of the leaves and stems in the background to generalized but accurate—and therefore believable—shapes.

Value helps differentiate forms and planes in painting in the same way detail can in a line drawing. Closer forms may be lighter, brighter, or darker than those far-

ther away from the viewer (Fig. 4-6). Experiment with this theory to see what brings your foreground closer and what pushes it back visually.

Availability

You do not have to go far to find a botanical subject no matter where you live. Step beyond your doorstep, and you will find dayflowers by the porch, dandelions dotting the lawn, chicory crowding a fire hydrant. You do not even have to step outside—nature is all around. Most of us grow houseplants year-round, and they make wonderful subjects (Fig. 4-7).

We tend to think working from nature requires a safari, a trip somewhere to find something really spectacular. The truth is that this beauty is to be found wherever we are (Fig. 4-8). Even in the inner city, there is a special poignancy in geraniums on a windowsill or the blue-sky blue of ''ragged soldiers,'' or chicory, growing in the cracks of the side-

4-6. The boldest values are used in the near flower to make it seem closest to the viewer. Notice how value changes give depth to the leaves as well. Untitled, by Peggy McKeehan. Reproduced courtesy of the artist.

4-7. I drew this philodendron with its harvestman occupant in my kitchen, using HB and 2B technical pencils.

4-8. Subjects for botanical drawings are often just outside our back door. This artist has found subjects for her delicate pen drawing in a basket of fall vegetables. *Harvest*, by Eileen James. Reproduced courtesy of the artist.

walk. When I lived in the city, I was surprised to find a wide variety of wild edibles within easy walking distance of my basement apartment—how many more plants would have been available to the artist, not the epicure, if I had been looking for them?

One of the things that makes rendering plants and flowers so satisfying is that they are so available, so *willing* to be drawn or painted. Unlike the deer that bounds away, white tail flicking in warning, or the bird that plays hide-and-seek in the leaves, plants will hold still and let you work to your heart's content.

4-9. The artist has discovered a strong graphic shape in this plant study. This piece is very effective, an unusual treatment for a botanical subject. *''Elsberry'' Autumn Olive*, by Terry Martin. Reproduced courtesy of the artist.

Observing and Drawing

Generally we need only to open our eyes and our minds to find a suitable subject. Then we need time to become acquainted. Once we discover what is around us, we need to slow down and choose which of this sudden wealth of subject matter most appeals to us at the time. What strikes an emotional chord, what glows with color or beguiles with a particular shape (Fig. 4-9). What captures just the mood we are after? It is helpful to spend a moment or two just sitting and looking at your subject, to decide from what angle you want to draw it or how close up you will be. Will you do a detailed study of one small plant, or a whole stand of purple loosestrife? Will you draw a flower or a cattail or wild grass?

If you can, first get close to your subject; use a hand lens if you like (Fig. 4-10). Know the plant you are drawing like a friend—let its particularity speak to you. The wonderful angular way a leaf joins a stem or the way some leaves enfold their stem like a garment at their bases, the way a flower invites easy pollination or hides its nectar like a secret reserved for only very special suitors to taste—the individual characteristics of

your subject, once seen, once experienced, will find their way into your work, making it real to you and to the viewer.

When we really see plants and flowers in all their diversity, we cannot help but be amazed at their beauty and variety. The tiny fog fruit is wonderfully different from the showy butterfly weed; the fresh rue anemones of spring, so very different from the hardy asters of autumn.

Find a simple plant to start with, a daisylike flower or an uncompli-

4-10. A spiky pencil stroke was used to express the character of the seeds of this wild grass. A hand lens helped me to examine the bristly seeds closely.

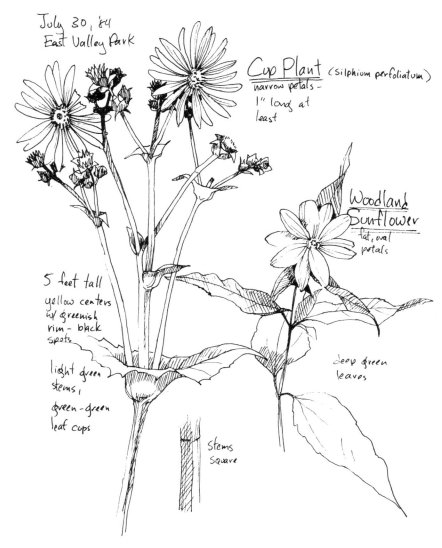

July 30, '84
East Valley Park

Cup Plant (silphium perfoliatum)
narrow petals -
1" long at
least

Woodland
Sunflower
flat, oval
petals

5 feet tall
yellow centers
w/ greenish
rim - black
spots

light green
stems,
green-green
leaf cups

deep green
leaves

Stems
Square

4-11. The differences in composition revealed by this close comparison of the cup plant and the sunflower—both golden daisylike summer flowers—amazed me. Modified contour drawing helped me get the shape of the "cup" right.

4-12. To find the correct perspective for any flower that fits into a disk shape, such as a daisy chrysanthemum, sunflower, or dandelion, draw the circumference *lightly* on your paper. (These were exaggerated for reproduction.) Draw the petals within the prescribed shape. Some variation will add liveliness. You may wish, instead, to make a dot where each petal meets an imaginary circle or oval, then draw your petals out to meet the dots.

cated green plant. Sit as comfortably nearby as possible. It is usually best not to pick the plant, not only because you may be uprooting an endangered species but because the subject will wilt and droop rapidly, losing the sense of life as you draw unless you are very quick indeed.

Try doing a modified contour drawing as you examine the plant's formation, its swellings and branchings (Fig. 4-11). It is strange that so little time is normally spent in getting to know what we draw. It can make such a difference. Our work rings true or echoes hollowly depending on how well we have seen, how deeply we have felt—and how carefully we allow our hand to follow our eyes. I have a tendency to look away from my subject and begin to concentrate for too long on my drawing instead, trying to make it look "right" or like a "work of art." There is, of course, a time for that, but often I find that, in looking away, in breaking contact with my subject for too long, I have been beguiled by the artificial and self-conscious lure of making my drawing look right. I am using symbols, substituting them for the real.

Of course we all *do* use symbols in our work—for grass or trees or twigs. Symbols are fine when used appropriately, and as long as I stay aware of what I am symbolizing in my drawing, it is okay. If I know what the plant I am abstracting really looks like, it will retain its integrity, its believability.

Unless you are looking straight down on a daisylike flower, the flower head will not describe a *perfect* circle. Draw instead a loose, light shape of the overall head on your paper: a circle for a flower you see straight on, an oval for one turned somewhat away from you, an almost straight line for one you see from an extreme side view (Fig. 4-12). Pay attention to their angles in relation to the side of the page. Now count the number of petals visible on the flower turned toward you, the ''circle'' shape. Check several other specimens to see if this particular plant *always* has a certain number of petals. Then begin to draw them in place around the flower's disk-floret center. Pay attention to how the center looks, how big it is, whether it looks smooth or rough. Draw the petals, keeping within the round shape you have drawn. Do the same thing when drawing foreshortened flowers that look oval or flat—it is not necessary to count the petals here, however, since they will not all be visible anyway. Some petals will overlap, some will tuck under—this variation adds life to your drawing. Add stems, leaves and buds, carefully observing your subject as you draw and keeping in mind which parts are closest to you, which are half-hidden behind other parts. When you are finished, erase the light circles and ovals that helped you keep your drawing in bounds.

When you are drawing more complicated flowers, such as roses or chrysanthemums, you may still want to outline the basic shape to help locate your drawing in the picture plane. But now you are faced with all those overlapping petals, confusing in their complexity. Look carefully to see if you can discern a pattern—a set number of

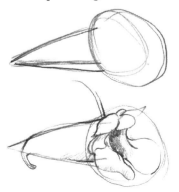

4-14. If it helps you to achieve the correct shapes, try fitting irregular flower shapes into geometric forms.

layers, perhaps, or a particular placement of petals. Do they alternate like shingles on a roof? Thinking of them in this way may help you place them correctly (Fig. 4-13). If there is a discernible pattern of layers, draw them lightly in place as you did the circumference. Succeeding layers will fall into place, but avoid a too rigidly geometric placement. Flowers usually have a certain asymmetry that gives them their special beauty. (One feature that makes plastic or silk flowers unpleasant is their perfection.) As you draw these more complicated flower shapes, draw first those things that are on top—petals closest to the center if you are drawing from above, or those closest the stem if you look from the side. This will help give your drawing depth. If you like, use heavier pressure where one petal folds under another to create shadow.

You may want to try breaking irregular flower shapes down into geometric shapes to draw them (Fig. 4-14). A jewelweed's trumpetlike flower might be drawn as an elongated cone with an oval shape at the large end. Refinements can then be made to conform the shape to reality. If this helps you, try it with other complicated or unusual shapes. I prefer to use a modified contour drawing and pretend my pencil is outlining the shape on the flower itself, as Clare Walker Leslie has done in her sketches in Figure 4-15. If the result is not entirely accurate, at least it seems to have more of a sense of life than when I go through an intermediate geometrical stage.

One of the hardest things to learn in drawing is simply to trust yourself. All the tools and tricks in the world, be they geometric shapes, tricks of perspective or form, are simply tools to help learn that one thing. If they can be bypassed, by all means do so. What your eyes can see, your

4-13. Look closely at this beautiful ink and watercolor painting, and notice how the flowers' petals overlap like shingles on a roof. The top petals were probably drawn first, then the petals beneath were added to give depth. Look also at the shapes of the flower heads and the sense of space the artist achieved with darker values in the foliage. *Chrysanthemums*, by Kitagawa Sosetsu (mid-seventeenth century). Reproduced by permission of the Nelson-Atkins Museum of Art, Kansas City, Missouri (Nelson Fund), gift of Mrs. George H. Bunting, Jr.

hand can draw—perhaps not with all the perfection of what you see before you, but certainly in a very satisfying way, recalling you to the time and place the drawing took form (Fig. 4-16).

Any good field guide will show you the amazing variety of flower and leaf shapes. Leaves may be

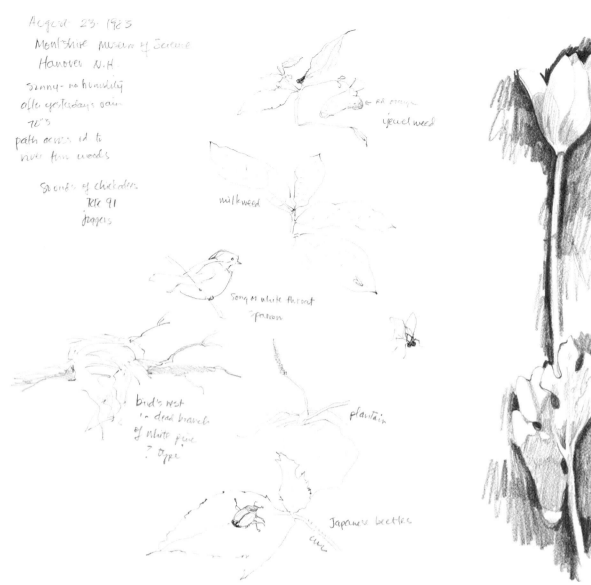

4-15. The artist has captured the sense of life in her quick sketch of the jewelweed on this field sketchbook page, as well as in the other subjects. She used a modified contour drawing to delineate these shapes. Sketchbook page, by Clare Walker Leslie. Reproduced courtesy of the artist.

4-16. Negative shapes helped explain the positive in this sketch of a bloodroot. A change in your way of "seeing" can give new life to your work. This drawing recalls me to the brilliant spring sunshine dappling the forest floor and striking pale fire where it touched the milky flowers.

4-17. A few of the leaf shapes found in nature.

4-18. When drawing complicated leaf shapes, a particularly useful exercise is to pretend your pencil point is an ant crawling over the leaf edges.

4-19. What says spring more clearly than the early wildflowers? These four technical-pen drawings of a trout lily, a sweet william, a trillium, and a dutchman's breeches were done as trail markers for the Martha Lafite Thompson Nature Sanctuary in Liberty, Missouri. Reproduced courtesy of the Sanctuary.

lance shaped, or round, fan shaped, with smooth margins, toothed margins, or lobed edges (Fig. 4-17). They may be simple, pinnately compound, or palmately compound. Consult a field guide for identification, but trust your eyes to draw believable leaf shapes. Practice simple shapes with pencil first, drawing the outer edge lightly, as you did the flower shapes; then add details—toothed margins, veins, or other modifications.

Drawing the mid-rib first may help you find the correct direction or shape for your leaf. This is the central vein of the leaf, and it is generally the heaviest one. Other veins often branch off from it, though not always. Some leaves have veins that radiate out from a central point; others have veins that run almost parallel to each other down their lengths, like lines on a superhighway. Observe carefully what your subject actually has. I draw the mid-rib first, if possible, to help me position the leaf in the picture plane. I complete the outside margin of the leaf, and then indicate other veins with lighter lines, following the overall perspective of the leaf. Observe where the leaf turns under or curves away and let your lines follow the curve. If it helps, think of the leaf as transparent. You will be able to "see" where the lines

follow the swell of the curve and can then continue it where it becomes visible again on the leaf tip. These curves are logical—their beginnings and ends do not just appear from nowhere. They are a continuation of what is happening on the visible plane.

To get a feeling of the roundness of the leaf as it curves, imagine yourself to be an ant on the surface (Fig. 4-18). Feel where the leaf swells, where it sinks near a rib or vein. Let your pencil be the ant.

Plants through the Seasons

Plants in one form or another are available as subjects year-round. Spring and summer are not the only times to go out and paint small plants and flowers, glorious though they may be (Fig. 4-19).

I look forward to the drought and heat of August, when the unrelieved, ubiquitous green of June and July begins to differentiate itself into greens touched with a hint of maroon, a bit of silver, a whisper of gold (Fig. 4-20). The sky bleaches almost to white where the sun burns brightest, and the weeds and grasses toast to shades of off-white and gold and sienna. The heat is unbearable later in the day, but a morning foray into ripening August makes finding the perfect plant to draw a real pleasure. In Septem-

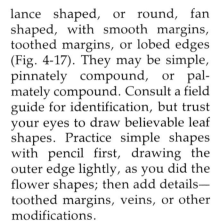

4-20. Silvery gray-green spurge is captured in this quick sketch. *Spurge*, by Keith Hammer. Reproduced courtesy of the artist.

March 23, '83

I was drawing these shelf fungus when a strange man came through the woods toward me. I felt like a deer in the woods — disappeared down the bank & across the creek!

4-22. These shelf fungi were drawn with a technical pencil in my field journal one early spring day. There is always something to draw outdoors, even if the flowers have not yet opened.

4-21. This seed-case study has a feeling of autumn and harvest about it. *Peppergrass*, by Cathy Johnson.

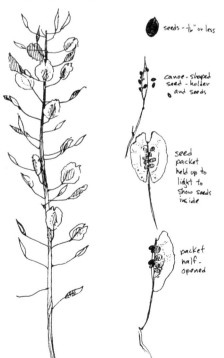

seeds - ⅛" or less

canoe-shaped seed-holder and seeds

seed packet held up to light to show seeds inside

packet half-opened

4-23. The pitted, convoluted cap of the morel was drawn with a crowquill pen. *Morchella esculenta*, by Cathy Johnson.

Morchella esculenta
Cathy Johnson

ber there are the glossy red fruits of jack-in-the-pulpit and the spiky, angular heads of Queen Anne's lace, dried to a rich brown. There are sumac's berries in dense, cone-shaped clusters, and a myriad golden sunflowers in bloom.

Studies of ripe grasses nodding their heavy heads and the seed cases of autumn and winter are equally interesting (Fig. 4-21). A rendering that reflects the changing shapes and shades of fall has a certain piquancy and power that an innocent summer painting lacks.

From the first tiny white Harbinger-of-Spring blooming in a protected place on a south-facing hill in February to the last aster of November, there is something to draw if you look for it. Keep a note with your sketches of the date and weather conditions, and you will have also created a learning tool and a record of your days.

4-24. This scratchboard drawing of a wildflower escapes sentimentality with a kind of lusty liveliness. By Ann Zwinger, in *Signs and Seasons*, by John Burroughs (Harper Colophon Books). Reproduced courtesy of the artist.

Mushrooms, Mosses, and Lichens

These unassuming small plants should be considered as subjects for rendering as well as the showier flowers and weeds. The coat of many colors worn by lichens on a damp rock makes an abstract pattern of jewellike complexity. Mosses are miniature forests, sere and brown when dry but brilliant acid green when touched with the least amount of moisture.

And, of course, there is the magical world of mushrooms and other fungi. Some years ago mushrooms were treated to an overdose of attention so intense that today it is difficult to portray them without slipping into cliché, but the effort to do so is well worth it. It forces us to *see*, to go beneath the surface of popularity and cute gnomelike caps to the mysterious realm of these saprophytic growths. Mushrooms and other fungi produce no chlorophyll, engage in no photosynthesis. They live off decaying matter and take wonderful, fantastic forms according to how and where and when they grow. Shelf

fungi, shown in Figure 4-22, grow on the sides of trees, old logs, rotting wood—one is even called artist's fungus because the clean, smooth underside was often used as a drawing surface.

Mushrooms grow during all seasons of the year, even in our yards and gardens. Again, note when and where you found your specimen; should you want to draw a particular variety again, it will be helpful to know in what season you might expect to find it if environmental factors have been favorable for growth. In a cold or dry spring, you will not find many morels such as that in Figure 4-23.

Flower Painting

Some time ago, in Victorian times, flowers seemed to be expressed most often in sickly sweet terms, sentimental and overdone. There is nothing wrong with *honest* sentiment, but this kind of rose-colored-glasses perfection did no favor to the viewer *or* the flower. Flowers were portrayed as perfect, and their actual awkward angles, tangled growth, insects, holes, and drought-curled edges were consequently disappointing. We aspired, perhaps, to heaven and neglected the wonder of life as it is. We rejected the gift.

It is useful to explore a variety of works and techniques to get beyond that desire for perfection bred by rosy sentimentality (Fig. 4-24). Abstraction is useful in this endeavor. The bare bones of the composition viewed in abstract terms are the framework on which to hang a painting (Fig. 4-25). Just because the subject is roses—or daisies or iris—does not mean that the underlying composition, the skeleton, cannot make a strong statement. For example, consider Oriental art. The flowers may be stylized or even appear stiff to our Western eyes, but the *reality*, the life, is there.

Some artists use a stark white background as a device to focus the eye on the flowers themselves, to set them apart from their environment. This creates strong patterns and interesting angles, as Figure 4-26 demonstrates.

4-25. The artist has used abstraction in his watercolor and pastel painting of leaves to express the complexity of nature. This same technique might be used to demythologize flower painting. Untitled, by Keith Hammer. Reproduced courtesy of the artist.

4-26. The white of the paper isolates these flowers, focusing the eye on the strong overall pattern. *Dutch Iris*, by Cathy Johnson.

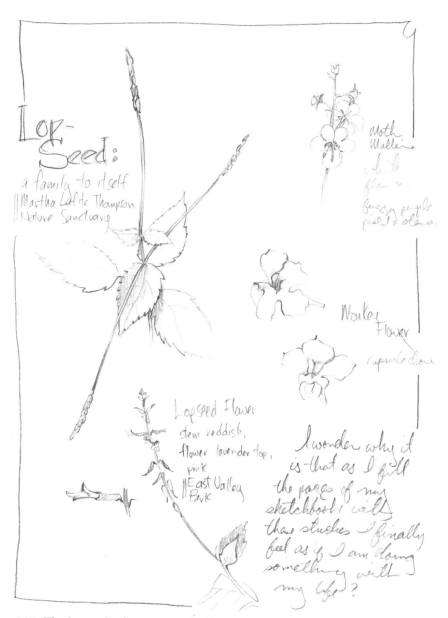

4-27. The lopseed's flowers practically require a hand lens to find.

It is not necessary—or even possible—to paint every stamen or vein on a plant. Simplification aids our eyes and our art. A confusing pattern of veins in a leaf can distract from the reality of that leaf. For the purposes of scientific illustration, such careful delineation may be necessary. Botanists, who must know the form of each midrib and vein, each lobe and indentation on a leaf, need such detailed information from a scientific standpoint; the average artist or illustrator does not. Emphasize the important points—and if you are working for publication (or simply want to), include at least one diagnostic detail, that is, one carefully drawn, recognizable leaf or flower, relatively flat to the picture plane. It is not necessary or even desirable to render every detail in this way. The effects of perspective and environmental factors come into play in either case for a sense of the real.

Celebrating the Nearly Invisible

In art as in life, the showy, the exciting, the high-profile, often catch our eye. Who can resist a vivid red rose or a royal purple ironweed? Who can pass up the butter-yellow cup plant or the orange butterfly weed? And indeed, why should you?

But there is another world, a smaller, more subtle, half-hidden world of miniatures, waiting to be discovered, like hobbit habitations just beyond our field of vision (Fig. 4-27). So low to the ground we need almost to crawl on hands and knees to see them, early spring henbits are an intricate delight of orchidlike beauty. Water horehound sports ruffs of tiny white flowers with tinier-still maroon spots. August's fog fruit hides in boggy places; it looks like minuscule vervain and belongs to the same family—visible only if we stop and take the time to see. And here, I think, is the real value in

4-28. Albrecht Durer's study of a small clump of wildflowers captures the tangled beauty of imperfection without sentiment. *Buttercups, Red Clover, and Plantain*, by Albrecht Durer. Reproduced by permission of the Museum of Art, Rhode Island School of Design, gift of Mrs. Margaret Bradley.

4-29. These pencil studies of tiny flowers and seed cases show us the beauty of these small wonders that we might miss if we move too fast. *Horse-nettle*, by Ann Zwinger, in *A Desert Country Near the Sea*, by Ann Zwinger (Harper and Row), 1983. Reproduced courtesy of the artist.

celebrating the nearly invisible: we stop, we take the time to experience. We see more fully that which we have to look hardest at in order to see at all. No quick once-over will suffice here. Riding by in a car or on a bike, we will miss this minute beauty altogether. Even at a fast walk, half of life goes by unseen. Awareness of these tiny jewels makes us stop and look and finally appreciate the hidden beauty all around us.

The artist helps us see. Albrecht Durer is well known for several of his studies of just this sort of subtle hidden beauty. His *Buttercups, Red Clover, and Plantain* celebrates this beauty and lets us share it too (Fig. 4-28). Nothing is too small—nothing is unworthy of our attention as artists and as living beings (Figs. 4-29 and 4-30).

4-30. The fruits or seeds of a tree are also interesting subjects for your paintings. The artist has perfectly captured the juicy roundness of these autumn fruits. *Pears*, by Eleanor Lewis. Reproduced courtesy of the artist.

CHAPTER FIVE

Trees and Shrubs

5-1

Trees are the largest plants on earth. In prehistoric times, ferns and other herbaceous plants grew to treelike stature, but gradually the woody behemoths of the forests were left as the only true trees. Druids worshipped them, and American Indians believed they were inhabited by nature spirits. And who is to say they were wrong? Who has not stood under a forest giant in the night, listening to the whisper of leaves and straining, just for a moment, to make out the message?

Trees mark the passing of our days and years in their growth. They are a part of our lives from earliest childhood: the day we finally gather the courage to climb cautiously into their leafy canopies and for the first time experience life from a different perspective—one not made by men—is impor-

tant to our own growth. We become aware of our "fellow" tree dwellers, the birds, mammals, and insects to whom this new world is as familiar as our own small beds. Later, as we learn about the varieties of trees and their uses, or perhaps gather nuts for a spectacular pecan pie or carry in wood for the fire, we see trees anew once again. If we maintain our childlike wonder, the naturalist's curiosity coupled with the artist's desire to express this serene, patient strength on paper or canvas, we will find in these forest denizens a special challenge (Fig. 5-2).

Tree Silhouettes
Using the vast variety of tree species in your work—judiciously, of course—will make it more in-

teresting and believable. As an exercise in becoming familiar with these woodland shapes, take every opportunity to record them in your sketchbook. These need not be detailed drawings of individual trees, simply outlines of the overall form (Fig. 5-3). These will not only provide you with invaluable research information for later works, but they will also give you a feeling for the myriad shapes trees within a single species can take. Of course, it is useful to have a diagnostic sketch of a particular variety on hand, but most real trees will not conform to this "typical" form: note how growing conditions, environment, and available moisture affect the tree shape. Prevailing winds, for example, are a factor in determining a tree's final form (Fig. 5-4). We are all familiar with the wind-

5-2. This study of a solitary tree captures the open laciness of the bare branches, an effect achieved with a fan brush. *Louis Vieux Elm*, by Jim Hamil. Reproduced courtesy of the artist.

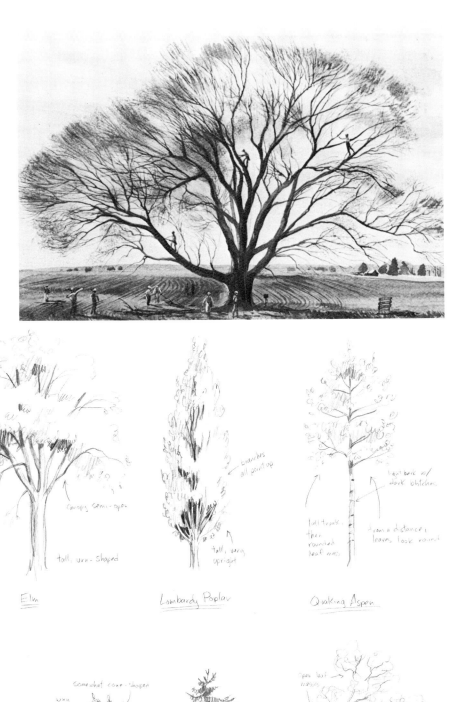

5-3. Go out into your neighborhood and make silhouette sketches of the various trees you find. Similar sketches can be made on a field trip to a new area to increase your tree "vocabulary." Reproduced courtesy of *The Artist's Magazine*.

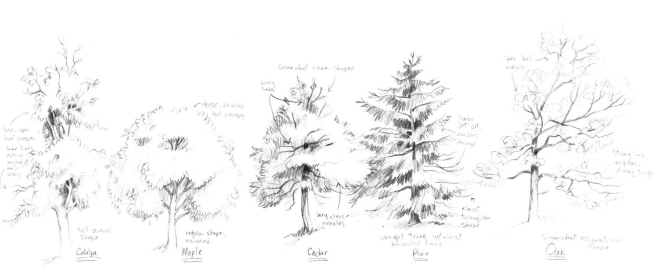

5-4. Look to see how prevailing winds affect a tree's shape as it grows. Such seemingly insignificant details will give your paintings and drawings a ring of truth. Reproduced courtesy of *The Artist's Magazine.*

5-5. This ink drawing of a gnarled tree conveys the harsh desert conditions it has endured. Untitled, by Eileen James. Reproduced courtesy of the artist.

twisted, gnarled mountain mesquite clinging to life in a hostile environment. Such trees have provided fascinating subjects for artists through the ages, symbolizing strength, perseverance, and character (Fig. 5-5). But *any* tree subject to constant winds will be affected in much the same way. Look at trees growing near the tops of hills or on an unprotected meadow: the canopy shape will be influenced as surely as that of an ancient mesquite on a canyon wall.

Density also affects tree shapes. When a tree grows alone in an open meadow, it can freely assume the shape for which its genes are programmed, given sufficient moisture and nutrients. But when that same tree sprouts instead in a crowded forest, it must compete for available light and food. It will grow first toward the light, often not putting out side shoots for 20 feet or more as it climbs toward the sun (Fig. 5-6). In dense woods, many trees hardly branch at all until they form an umbrella of limbs near the overall canopy of the forest. If you are depicting a scene within a

dense forest, remember that while the forest giants may be quite normal in shape because they were first on the scene and received much more available light, the younger trees may appear almost branchless, slender and delicate. In a windstorm, such trees will sway visibly almost to their roots—that is, the trunk will move slightly even at nearly ground level.

Individual Trees

Individual trees are good subjects for studies. Some patience and a sense of depth of field are required to capture them with life and vigor. Look at which limbs come toward you, which recede. How can you express a sense of roundness, of taking up of actual three-dimensional space? Shadows help here. Use the light to help you depict roundness and shape, not only to show the volume of the trunk itself but to explain the position of branches and their relationship to each other (Fig. 5-7).

5-6. This sketch of a tree in dense woods shows how far a trunk may grow before it branches when it must compete for available sunlight. A painting of a woodsy interior might include a number of these slender trunks.

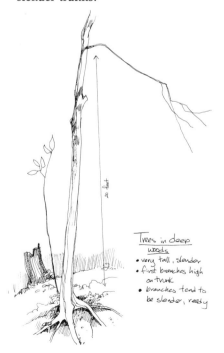

Trees in deep woods
• very tall, slender
• first branches high on trunk
• branches tend to be slender, ready

C-1. Sketching is an invaluable aid to planning any piece of artwork. Here, I took a longer view of the tree first (a), then zeroed in for a more intimate study (b). The colors were accurate but dead flat, so I tried one more time for a livelier effect (c).

C-2. I was happiest with (c), the final sketch, so I used it to capture the wonderful old bent tree in strong sunlight. Notice the variations in shape and size in the negative areas.

C-3. In this detail, notice how the texture is suggested using wet-on-wet technique, glazes, dry-brush technique, and a bit of fine-line calligraphy. *Ancient Tree in Sun*, 15 by 22 inches, watercolor on cold-press paper.

C-4. Hot-press watercolor paper was used for this study of planes and textures of redstone formations in the Valley of Fire in Nevada. Pigment tends to puddle on the surface of this slick paper, creating interest. Several designers and illustrators are using this ultrasmooth surface to obtain fresh effects.

C-5. Notice the varieties of textures and techniques in this detail. I used spatter, lifts, scraping, and a bit of linear work with my fan brush to suggest the weathered stones. *Redstone,* 15 by 22 inches, watercolor on hot-press paper.

C-6. Building layers of color
can suggest great detail and
depth, even on a small scale.
Here, the first light washes
are laid down with a large
brush, a no. 10 red-sable
round.

C-7. With the same large
brush, the middle values are
added to define forms
further.

C-8. Only for the final fine details do I switch
to a smaller, no. 4 brush. *Shelf Fungus*, 9 by
12 inches, watercolor on cold-press paper.

C-9. Shapes are carefully drawn to capture the jack-in-the-pulpit, and first washes are laid down. Notice the masking tape used to define edges and separate sides of the diptych.

C-11. I paid attention to the patterns of light and dark as I developed the ''spring'' side of this diptych and kept the negative shapes interesting and varied.

C-10. Middle values are built up after the first washes are thoroughly dry to keep everything fresh. If I had put them in earlier, they might have lifted and muddied the underwashes.

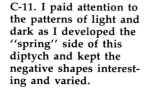

C-12. The completed painting is a botanical study not only of a specific plant, but of the passing of the seasons. *Jack-in-the-pulpit Diptych*, 15 by 22 inches, watercolor on cold-press paper.

C-13. Trees have varied personalities and can be handled in many ways to capture the effects you want. This color sketch was done on the spot. *Tree Sketch*, 12 by 16 inches, graphite and water-color on vellum-surface paper.

C-14. Watercolorist Jim Hamil has created a wonderful portrait of a very specific tree. Notice the use of the fan brush in the rough grasses and the small twigs in the background. *Sycamore, Late Afternoon*, 15 by 22 inches, watercolor on paper.

C-16. Artist/naturalist Gordon Morrison has done a study of pine trees and rocks that communicates a totally different mood than my sketch in Figure 5-3 does. Gordon applies acrylics using a watercolor technique. *Pine Trees and Rocks*, 11 by 14 inches, acrylic wash on illustration board.

C-15. Trees in a landscape are handled graphically in this acrylic by J. L. McKeehan. Many tiny dots of pigment suggest light-struck leaves. *Gathering*, 18 by 28 inches, acrylic on board.

C-17. Household pets make wonderful subjects and often seem quite willing to pose. Here I have included a snapshot and a rough sketch along with my original attempt.

C-19. Here you can see that the corrections were made without being obvious—in spite of what people say about watercolor being an unforgiving medium. This pose is much more characteristic of my cat; familiarity with my subject supplemented by a number of sketches enabled me to make believable improvements. *Reuben Goldstein*, 15 by 22 inches, watercolor on cold-press paper.

C-18. The back seemed wrong in spite of the clear evidence of the photo, and I had overlooked my cat's back foot in my haste. I wetted the area again and lifted out a light foot, then softened the line of the back with clear water; I washed in the new configuration while the area was still damp.

C-20. Animals can be painted in any number of ways, using various media. Gordon Morrison has done a careful study, applying acrylic using a watercolor technique.

C-21. Fur or hair can be handled quite simply, as you can see in this detail of my *Arrowrock Goats*. Light-struck body contours were lifted with a damp tissue while the pigment was still wet, and a few ''hairs'' were scraped into the wet wash.

C-22. Goats have body characteristics similar to those of other ungulates (hoofed animals) such as deer, elk, and antelope. Practice painting what is close at hand. *Arrowrock Goats*, 15 by 22 inches, watercolor on cold-press paper.

C-23. Bob Salo's oil captures the inherent wildness in the elusive cougar. Notice the wonderful, asymmetrical composition that breaks the rules with elan; you *feel* the cougar about to leap out of the picture plane. Background sketches and photos are invaluable when painting wildlife, especially animals as shy of man as the American mountain lion. *Watchful Eye*, 18 by 30 inches, oil on canvas.

C-24. Artist/naturalist Clare Walker Leslie used colored pencils to sketch this landscape study of her ridge in Vermont. Notice the wide range of tonal values possible with this versatile medium; pencils are quite portable and invaluable to an artist who works outdoors much of the time. *Landscape Sketch*, 8 by 10 inches, colored pencils and felt-tip pen.

C-25. Acrylics were laid on in flat, smooth applications for an almost mosaic effect in this painting by John Stewart. John mixes small batches of paint in film cans with snap-on lids to keep them for later use. *New Mexico Clouds*, 14 by 18 inches, acrylic on board.

C-26. Here Keith Hammer used acrylics in a very different manner; the application of color is both looser and thinner than in Figure C-25. *Farm Pond*, 18 by 24 inches, acrylic on board.

5-7. This exquisite watercolor of a sycamore demonstrates the use of light and shade to depict roundness as well as the branching and narrowing of limbs as the trunk diminishes. The artist has used foreshortening to give a feeling of depth. *White Sycamore*, by Frederic James. Reproduced courtesy of the artist and by permission of the Nelson-Atkins Museum of Art, Kansas City, Missouri (Anonymous gift).

They will throw their shadows across the trunk and each other—look to see how you can show that branching in a believable way. See also how limbs become progressively smaller as they branch, and how the trunk is reduced in size proportionate to that branching. Many artists paint a trunk as if it were the same diameter from ground to top, and limbs are often depicted much too large to allow such uniformity. Look at what is before you and think how the blood vessels in the human body branch and narrow until they end in tiny capillaries. Tree limbs, branches, and twigs work in much the same way.

The understory or shrub level of a forest will contain many immature trees as well as those trees and bushes that will never attain great height. At this level, in midwestern woods, one often sees young buckeye trees, their leaves disproportionately large like the feet of an adolescent, intermixed with smaller, mature redbud and dogwood, like that shown in Figure 5-8, and a variety of brushy plants such as sumac and elderberry.

Individual trees within a species can give a feeling for the vast variety of shapes possible, for light

5-8. Midwestern woods are full of small trees such as redbud and dogwood. Variety makes your work believable and interesting. *Dogwood*, by Cathy Johnson, © 1983 by the National Wildlife Federation, in *National Wildlife Magazine*, June/July 1983. Reproduced courtesy of the National Wildlife Federation.

and growing conditions, for life itself. One tree, one special, individual tree, can represent many (Fig. 5-9). One tree, seen truly, can express all "treeness" to the viewer.

Choose a special tree and become intimately acquainted with it. If you are like most of us, you probably already have a special tree or two—one you pass often or see throughout all its seasonal changes, one that holds a nest of young birds you have watched as a family through territorial claims, courtship, and nest building, or perhaps one that reminds you of a favorite climbing tree from your youth. Perhaps you love pines or oaks or apple trees—choose your favorite and draw it over and over, in all seasons. You will be a better and more sensitive artist for this discipline.

5-9. This sensitive study of a particular pine tree symbolizes all pine trees to me. Pen-and-ink and pencil were painstakingly applied to convey the soft feeling of the pine needles. *Pine Tree*, by Charles Herbert Moore. Reproduced by permission of the Art Museum, Princeton University, Princeton, New Jersey, gift of Elizabeth Huntington Moore.

Bark Patterns

Make studies of bark patterns in your sketchbook. Bark protects the tree's food-conducting phloem layer, which carries nutrients down from the leaves, where they are produced, to other parts of the tree. In addition, it provides a home for a variety of insects and food for a number of creatures as well.

Each tree species has a type of bark uniquely suited to its mode of survival. The texture of bark results as the inner stem grows, splitting the inelastic bark cells to form patterns characteristic of the species. The texture of sycamore bark is paperlike, flaking off later in the growing season in great curved strips to expose gleaming white upper limbs. Oak bark is deeply ridged and as strong as the tree itself. Elm bark is corky, beech is smooth and fleshlike, and shagbark hickory looks as if it were about to burst, shedding bark in all directions. A page or two of various bark patterns in your sketchbook will be a useful refer-

5-10. Bark studies.

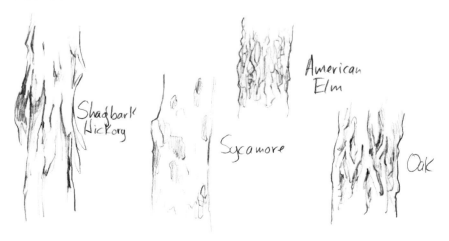

5-11. This watercolor painting of late-fall leaves and berries was a contemplative exercise. *Linden, Ornamental Plum, and Wahoo (or Spindleberry)*, by Cathy Johnson, © 1987. Reproduced courtesy of Prentice-Hall Press, Inc.

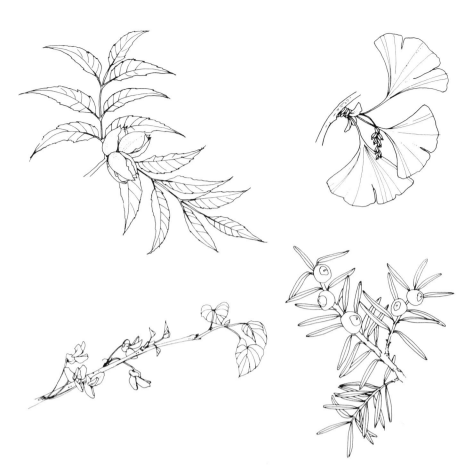

5-12. Close studies of leaves, fruit, and flowers, as in this technical-pen drawing, will help give you a sense of how to render an entire tree, though you may never need such detail. Leaf study, by Cathy Johnson. Reproduced courtesy of the Kansas City, Missouri, Board of Parks and Recreation Commissioners.

ence, even if you never do a painting so detailed (Fig. 5-10). It will give your work a depth that a background of understanding provides. Of course, if you do natural history or scientific illustration, such studies are invaluable.

Leaves

The same value gained from studying bark patterns can also be obtained from a study of leaves (Figs. 5-11 and 5-12). Again, the type and shape of leaf is determined by the needs of the particular tree species. A white pine has an entirely different leaf from a cottonwood—as does, of course, an oak or elm or walnut. They are not only quite different on close inspection but will also look different when viewed as part of the overall forest community. From a distance a pine may have an almost hazy, diaphanous look at some seasons. At other times it will appear thunderously dark and vivid against a snowy background. An oak's leaves, growing as they often do in rounded

5-13. The artist has captured the lacy, open feel of these creekside aspens using round, dotlike strokes that mirror the shape of the leaves themselves. This somewhat abstract composition has a feeling of reality. (See Fig. C-15 in the color section for a color reproduction of this painting.) *Gathering*, by J.L. McKeehan. Reproduced courtesy of the artist.

5-14. This sketch and watercolor progression demonstrates an interesting way to express a stand of young trees by capitalizing on light and dark to give a sense of depth. Notice the simplified shapes that still perfectly express the light-struck edge of the woods. *Trees*, by Roberta Hammer. Reproduced courtesy of the artist.

clumps, look quite different—even from a distance—from a redbud's overlapping, broad, heart-shaped leaves or the lacy, open tops of walnuts. This variety, even when only hinted at in the final work, gives a sense of life (Fig. 5-13). Observe how richly dark an oak's leaves appear, while a sycamore's glossy leaves contain more golden lights. Later in the season, when the unchanging greens of May and June and July start to differentiate themselves in August's heat, these color differences are even more apparent. Look carefully and use what you see. Even in a golden aspen grove, an occasional dark mountain pine will punctuate the glow.

There are a number of techniques available to the watercolorist to capture the feel of a leaf canopy. A wet-in-wet technique will give a soft haziness reminiscent of early morning or a rainy day. A sponge can be used to paint leaf masses, but be sure to vary the application so your leaves do not appear uniform and stamped-on. Turn your sponge so that different areas are in contact with your paper. Scumbling, a rough, loose technique of brush handling perhaps more familiar to oil painters, can also be used by watercolorists to hint at broken, lacy leaf masses. A few characteristic leaf shapes at the edges of these masses where they would naturally appear in silhouette help to simplify and describe various species without the need to paint each leaf—a prodigious task considering leaves may number in the millions!

To give your tree canopies a sense of volume, do not forget the effects of light discussed in the

5-15. This pastel painting illustrates a particularly effective use of holes punched in the tree canopy to reveal the dappled light of the sky. *Miller's Crossing*, by Donna Aldridge. Reproduced courtesy of the artist.

5-16. Notice how some "holes" in a tree's canopy go only part way through. The shadowy interior is visible, as are limbs, twigs, and undersides of leaves.

5-17. The use of artful shading and a strong value pattern keep this carefully rendered scene from appearing overworked. *Landscape with Cattle, 1846*, by George Caleb Bingham. Reproduced by permission of the St. Louis Art Museum, St. Louis, Missouri (Gift of Mrs. Chester Harding Krum).

section on individual trees. Light affects everything we see, giving it definition, and helps our eyes to perceive depth and detail (Fig. 5-14). Think again of the hour just before dawn, when everything looks flat, two-dimensional, before the light defines shapes and creates shadows.

Some trees will reflect the light with golden yellows on light-struck sides, whereas others with shiny leaves may bounce back the cool blue of the sky. "Local color," the true, unaffected color of an object, is visible when leaves are illuminated but not necessarily directly light-struck, and shadowed areas may be cooled with blue, purple, or black. Jim Hamil is particularly good at seeing—and therefore depicting—the elusive back lighting of the setting sun. He lights the edges of the leading trees with burnt sienna, a simple but wonderfully effective device. Color, used judiciously, gives life, a sense of reality, to your work.

5-18. The artist has used three basic planes in this watercolor to keep a forest scene readable. A complex subject is nevertheless understandable in this piece through careful use of value and depth. *Virgin Land*, by Jim Hamil. Reproduced courtesy of the artist.

5-19 and 5-20. It is interesting to see how two different artists have handled a similar subject, a winter forest bare of leaves. In each case a strong value pattern, somewhat abstracted, is used to maintain the overall essence of the subject. (See also Fig. 5-14 for an example of a wooded hillside painted in summer near the location of Fig. 5-19.) 5-19: *Winter Hill*, by Roberta Hammer; 5-20: *Hills, Trees and Sky*, by Maria Alfie. Reproduced courtesy of the artists.

Punching Holes

You can paint tree masses with open areas stitched together with dark limbs, a valid approach, if that is what you see (Fig. 5-15). More often, when you look at a tree, the "hole" will go only partway through the tree canopy, revealing not the light sky behind but the shadowed depths of the tent of leaves (Fig. 5-16). These holes are like windows into the infrastructure generally hidden by the leaves, revealing the branches and stem, the skeleton of the tree normally noticed only when deciduous trees have dropped their leaves in the fall. Like the struts and beams of an ancient barn, these branches help make sense of the outer shape. Some will appear dark and shadowed, others will catch the light. Punching a simplified "hole" in the foliage gives a sense of that skeleton, and of the dimension and depth of the tree. It also will keep your tree from looking like a green lollipop.

Some trees, of course, have such a dense leaf canopy that no such holes *can* logically be punched in them—so don't. Variety spices art as well as life.

Lost in the Woods

Attempting to depict a scene within dense or even open woods can be confusing and intimidating—so much is happening. In this case it often helps to think in terms of a series of planes. Background, middle ground, and foreground apply here just as they do in more straightforward landscape painting; they are just a bit more difficult to discern.

Try wearing dark, polarized glasses, looking through a piece of transparent colored plastic, or even squinting your eyes to help you see these planes. Use thumbnail sketches or value sketches to help you fix them in your mind. You *cannot* paint every detail in the forest—although some artists have seemed to (look at the work of Albert Bierstadt or George Caleb Bingham, as in Figure 5-17, for some amazing examples of detail). If you are happiest rendering these incredible intricacies and can still maintain a sense of depth, composition, and just plain interest, you do not need my warnings. Those who, like me, achieve only a dead over-working when too beguiled by detail, may be helped—in some instances at least—by a trick of John Pike's; it is certainly worth a try to help organize and educate your mind and eye when faced with too much richness.

Keep the background simple and fairly light, to give a sense of distance. Remember, atmospheric haze often blues and flattens distant objects. The middle ground might be darker and shadowed, as trees within deep woods often are. Then the foreground or center of interest can be quite detailed, perhaps light-struck here and there to help lead the eye into the picture. Try it—it very often makes sense and feels right (Fig. 5-18).

Seeing the Forest

Here the situation is just the opposite of that above—we are on the outside looking in instead of within the confusing interior (Figs. 5-19 and 5-20). How can we give a sense of a tree-covered hillside without making it look like a collection of green marshmallows? Again, the color differentiation discussed earlier will help clarify images. Remember that on a hillside, whole trees shade each other, not just individual leaf masses. These leaf masses must be downplayed in deference to the interlocking shapes of the trees themselves. Help them stand out from each other not just with color but also with the use of shadows to define shapes and planes (Fig. 5-21). You will be able to see some

5-21. To depict a view into the forest, a flat drawing or carpenter's pencil was used to create overall values to differentiate mass and planes.

5-22. Using a simple nylon-tipped pen can suggest great variations in light and shade.

dark-shadowed trunks and a few of the larger limbs, while some limbs will be light-struck or shine with their own eerie light, such as the pale upper limbs of sycamore trees and birches. (Remember that sycamores love water and will be found most often at lower levels of a wooded hillside where a

stream would most likely flow.)

These details should not be overworked or labored (Fig. 5-22). A slight suggestion of shapes and shadows, light and dark, may be enough to give the impression of a forest community while retaining the freshness of your original vision.

CHAPTER SIX

Rocks and Other Geological Wonders

6-1

The earth was originally molten, lifeless rock. Through the millennia, the stresses of wind and weather, temperature extremes, and the slow—or rapid—changes of position of the great plates thrown up by the settling of the earth's crust have molded and changed the rock. Mountains were formed when the plates shifted and ground against each other, and ranges were then weathered, gentled by the insistent, irresistible forces of wind and ice and blown sand, wearing away their angles and edges until these older mountains became smooth and rounded. Newer ranges such as the Rockies are still angular, dramatic in their primeval harshness, while in the Grand Canyon,

the forces of water and erosion have carved their names in the walls and changed the land forever (Fig. 6-2). Wherever we live, rocks tell a story of the passing of eons, and they can form the foundation of our paintings (Fig. 6-3). Landscapes need not be all pastoral scenes, sentimental and inviting; some are dramatic, otherworldly, composed of fantastic shapes and shadows.

As rock weathered and changed, smaller boulders, rocks, and pebbles were broken off, and these in turn began their long, slow transformation. Some were in creek beds, where the constant flow of water tumbled and rounded them. Some were slowly penetrated by lichens, and in the

tiny resulting crevices, water entered, froze, and expanded, further breaking them apart.

Some rocks emerged when great volcanoes erupted, formed by the slowly hardening lava flow; you can't help but paint them with a certain sinuous hint of frozen motion. Others were formed by billions of years of pressure exerted on clay or mud. Fossils were imprisoned in this way, showing us something about life in another age (Fig. 6-4). You may think of rocks as lifeless and inert, scarcely interesting subjects for rendering, but geology opens our eyes to the romance hidden in the stones. Their beauty and variety is incredible. Visit any rock shop to see the many shapes and colors and

6-2. This dramatic oil done in 1912 captures the effects of weathering and shifting lights on the canyon walls. The artist has used diminished detail and lighter colors to give the effect of distance. *Grand Canyon*, by Thomas Moran. Reproduced by permission of the Nelson-Atkins Museum of Art, Kansas City, Missouri (Nelson Fund).

6-3. Values were explored to express depth in this pencil study.

types of rocks found even in a small locale. Worldwide, these stones are as varied and beautiful. These "lifeless and inert" rocks, after all, once burst with a roar and a blinding light from the heart of a star.

Textures and Techniques

Rocks and other geological formations have many textures, de-pending on how they came about, so a variety of techniques for rendering them should be mastered. Some rocks are rough and jagged, some are smoothed by water and time, others are sandy, as if a child's sandbox had hardened.

The technique that you choose will depend largely upon what medium you use to express the texture. If you are working in pen-cil, texture can be built up gradually and carefully; pay particular attention to the light source and how it affects the visible surface (Fig. 6-5). You can allow your pen-cil to follow surface cracks, varying pressure on the lead to give the feeling of deepening or widening of the cracks (Fig. 6-6). Dots can be built up to express surface pitting or the varied specks of feld-spar, mica, and quartz in a gran-

6-4. In this watercolor I attempted to explore the various textures of the rocks found around Missouri. Two were fossilized types of mud, one bore tiny shell fossils, one was flint, and one was limestone worn completely through by water. This study forced me to try to show that some surfaces were smooth; others, pitted; still others, broken off in shards. *Rock Varieties*, by Cathy Johnson.

6-5. A very smooth pencil technique was used here to express the feeling of water-polished rocks. Tones were patiently built up with overlapping strokes of HB lead.

proach, treating these forms almost as a still life. Pebbles in a streambed form intricate patterns, challenging to the artist (Fig. 6-8).

The stark black-and-white of pen-and-ink can effectively capture the hard, nearly impenetrable quality of your subject, if not, perhaps, the subtleties of light and dark. But there are a variety of ways to express these strong shapes with the bold medium of india ink. A strictly chiaroscuro effect may satisfy you as you look at the strong shadows of summer on a rock ledge. Try filling in the shadows with solid shapes of black, as if only the two values of black and white were visible, and see how you capture the stark character you see before you. Early morning or late afternoon is the best time to see this effect in nature, when the shadows are long and bold. Smaller details may then be added if you wish, but they are unnecessary to your overall composition. A thumbnail sketch can be of use here as it is in other works; careful planning is the key.

This strong black-and-white effect is particularly well suited to scratchboard, the clay-coated pa-

6-6. A number of pencil techniques were used to render this little rock: linear strokes, rough zig-zag lines to express shadows, dots and stippling. It was an interesting exercise in value as well as technique. Notice the different effect technique produces, as compared to the effect produced by the building of tones in Fig. 6-5.

ite surface. Light brings out the shape and character of rock forms as it does that of all visible things. Use this knowledge to give your work a sense of volume and strength. Chiaroscuro, the play of light and dark, can deliver a dramatic commentary on the massive shapes before you in such places as Arizona's Monument Valley and Missouri's Elephant Rocks.

Almost every part of the world boasts places where the ribs of rock layers show through, mute reminders of the passing of glaciers, prehistoric inland seas, or centuries of erosion (Fig. 6-7). You can express these bedrock forms with pencil, using quick, jagged strokes of the point to depict the ruggedness you see. Or you may prefer a more contemplative apper that allows for inking in solid shapes and then altering them when dry by scratching into the surface and through the thin ink layer to expose the white underneath. White-on-black effects unobtainable by other methods are easy to achieve in scratchboard (Fig. 6-9).

You can also use stippling to express areas of halftone. You can achieve all the subtlety of a pencil drawing or a painting if you persevere.

Many artists use a series of lines or cross-hatching to depict the forms and textures of rocks. If it captures the essence of rock for you, try it. In Figure 6-10 Mary Leathers used parallel lines to show the directional planes of the rocks in a streambed. This effectively gives the feeling of flat rocks piled against and jumbled with one another, a typical sight at streamside.

The midwest is blessed with a variety of rock forms. High in the woods, one often sees an exposed cliff, perhaps moss covered and dripping water from an underground stream. The Missouri Ozarks abound with spectacular rock formations of the sort one

6-7. Vigorous ink lines were used to capture the rocky bluffs of the canyon walls and bright sunlight of this arid land. Look closely to see how the artist's strokes follow the planes of the canyon. *Bright Angel Trail, Indian Gardens, Grand Canyon*, by Gary Gretter. Reproduced courtesy of the artist.

might expect to see only in the west, and along the Missouri and Mississippi rivers, limestone cliffs rise to dizzying heights (Fig. 6-11). Fossils, often found, fascinate and inspire the artist/naturalist. (Nature's designs are among the most elegant.) Rocky streambeds web the land as if a giant aquatic spider had been at work.

Watercolor can wonderfully capture this texture and angular-

ity. There are a number of ways to build up rocklike textures, using straight painting techniques or watercolor tricks. Salt added to a wash makes a sandy texture, as does sawdust or other granular additives. India ink worked into a wet wash will dance off into cracks or fissures (see Fig. 3-16). Glazes may be patiently built up to express the colors of stratified rock or the accretions of mosses

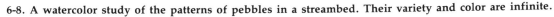

6-8. A watercolor study of the patterns of pebbles in a streambed. Their variety and color are infinite.

6-9. Chiaroscuro—the use of light and dark—creates the drama in this ink drawing on scratchboard. (a) Notice how the shadows form the frame on which the composition is hung. The darks were carefully designed and painted in india ink with an old watercolor brush. (b) I began scratching into the solid blacks with a variety of tools after the ink was *thoroughly* dry (whites will not be white on scratchboard if you try to work back into your composition too soon—allow several hours between steps, if possible). Two kinds of scratchboard tools were used, plus a needlelike tool for fine details. When I found I had removed too much of the black in an area, I simply restored it with ink until I achieved the effect I wanted.

6-10. The artist has used parallel lines to show the planes of the rocks in this lithograph.
Rocks I, by Mary Leathers. Reproduced courtesy of the artist.

and lichens, water stains, or stalactites.

Geology for the Artist

Borrow or buy a good book on geology or enroll in an adult-education class to see the subject in a new way. It is interesting from a scientific or even historical point of view—but let it speak to you as an artist as well. Read what made these forms as they are, and then try squinting your eyes as you look at the pictures to see abstract forms hidden in them. Consider them as shapes to be manipulated into your own compositions, colors to be borrowed for their harmony or drama (Fig. 6-12). Envision how those stratified layers of agate could be—with a bit of imagination—a desert collage or a painted mesa (Fig. 6-13).

Mineral forms are intricate as well, inspiring the artist or designer with visions of enchanted caves and jewels beyond price. The colors contained in crystalline and cryptocrystalline quartz and the gem minerals rival the prismatic hues of the rainbow. Let your imagination have free rein. These inorganic, and stable, chemical elements are the foundation of the earth itself.

In the field, try this: touch that rocky cliff face, run your hands over a granite boulder, pick up a handful of cool, smooth pebbles. Smell them—taste them! Then let this childlike wonder pervade your work. We often miss what is right before us as we rush about our lives—let your work show others, help them to stop and see.

Mountains, Cliffs, Bluffs, and Hills

Large natural forms are more monumental than those we have considered previously, but they are of equal interest to the artist (Fig. 6-14). These elements are contained in traditional land-

6-11. This pencil drawing of an abandoned limestone quarry was done on a cloudy day.

6-12. I was as interested in showing the effects of light as I was the texture of the rock in this pencil drawing of a granite boulder.

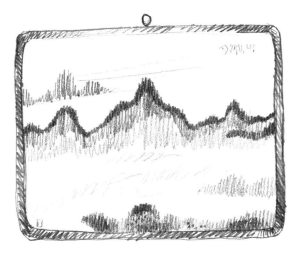

6-13. A slab of marble contains an autumn scene for those who can see it. This slab is from an ancient set of Chinese natural marble ''paintings,'' untouched by man.

6-15. In these folded hills in shadow, drawn with china marker on coquille board, I have tried to show the rounded quality of the glacial hills.

6-14. Pen-and-ink effectively expresses the starkness of the subject. Analyze how the artist has used his strokes to depict the character of the rock faces. *Gorge of the Little Colorado River*, by Gary Gretter. Reproduced courtesy of the artist.

scapes, but a bit of background knowledge of how they were formed and why they look the way they do can lend your work a ring of truth. When you draw a windswept bluff, exposed for centuries, weathered by ice and wind, try to capture that weathering. Try to get inside your subject. Hills like those in Figure 6-15 may be softly rounded after eons of erosion, a gradual wearing away or building up of forms—imagine you are riding an eagle's wings and see them from the air. Imagine you are big enough to stroke them with your hand—how would they feel? Let that show in your work.

CHAPTER SEVEN

The Landscape

7-1

Visit any of the great museums of the world, and you will see the two perennially favorite subjects of the great artists: the human figure and the landscape. The depiction of landforms helps us to place ourselves on earth in our own minds, to imagine ourselves there, to see places we have never been or revisit places we love. We may travel in time and space, see history come alive, explore the mysteries of fantastic lands that never saw the light of our sun. We may see these works as explanations of habitat or as uninhabited dreamscapes. Like the human figure, landscapes touch a deep chord within us.

Throughout history artists have been inspired by these natural forms. Vincent van Gogh saw his environment through eyes that were touched, perhaps, by madness, but he produced some of the most affecting paintings ever made by the hand of man. Rembrandt sketched his native land over and over in tiny drawings, leaving us a legacy of almost sensory works, life captured in line. Paul Gauguin painted his adopted tropical island home. J. M. W. Turner showed us his England, as did Thomas Gainsborough and John Constable. Paul Cézanne, Peter Paul Rubens, and Raoul Dufy shared their visions with the ages—we can do likewise.

We need not measure our efforts by those of the masters: we are not in competition with them.

We *share* their vision. As watercolorist Frederic James says, ''I work only from life; my own personal visual experience. To me there is no other way. Although I owe a great debt to artists of the past, everything I do as an artist is my own, of my own life, of my own experiences, of my own feelings about life. I do not use mechanical equipment of any kind and by doing so feel that I am closer to reality. Perhaps it is self-indulgence, but my greatest pleasure is in feeling close to nature while drawing or painting.'' It is in the trying, in the time spent in the experience, that the greatest value lies. The end product is often unimportant. An individual work may be transient—it may

7-2. The artist has attempted to capture a complex pattern of leaves, shredding sycamore bark, and an old farmhouse, using color and value to make sense of the composition. Oil, by Terry Martin. Reproduced courtesy of the artist.

end up in the trash bin or relegated to the back of a closet, but the experience of being out in nature, of seeing, of feeling, of smelling the rich fragrance of breeze and flower and spice-scented weed and dying leaves—that is with us forever. If we are lucky, a part of that experience will translate itself to the paper; if we are lucky, we will be able to share with our viewers a sense of that moment.

An Overall View

Landscapes are generally thought of as wide vistas, scenic panoramas. This does not necessarily have to be the case, of course—many of my own paintings are what I call ''intimate landscapes,'' almost still lifes, not arranged by human hands. But first, let us consider the traditional landscape with which we are most familiar. A landscape gives a sense of spaciousness, of perspective and distance. It can be a single scene with few elements or an intricate interweaving of forms and shapes and colors, depending on where you are and how you see what is before you (Fig. 7-2). The scene itself may be busy, with hills, trees, rocks, streams, and so forth tumbling all over each other with no apparent rhyme or reason. But if you like, you can pick and choose those elements you will include, change directions and angles at will to form a better composition, even change weather conditions or the season (Fig. 7-3).

This is one advantage the artist has over the nature photographer. Whereas photographers must work with only what is before

7-3. The artist has chosen to simplify this composition by using repeated strokes to suggest ice-covered winter grasses in this pastel landscape. She tells of finding herself in a ''fairy-tale world of sugar-frosted landscapes with gossamer skies. Tree branches were transformed into glistening crystal sculptures and long grasses arched their heads over to earth, heavy with the thick coating of ice.'' *Frost Morning*, by Donna Aldridge. Reproduced courtesy of the artist.

7-4. Format and value sketches can help you plan a painting. Eventually I used the top left sketch because of its dynamic wave pattern.

format & value sketches for a sooscape

them, adjusting by camera angle, aperture, time, or special lenses, artists may take what they see and transform it into a medieval garden or a moonscape or simply a more pleasing arrangement of what they see.

The sketchbook is an invaluable tool here. Unless what you see strikes such a chord that you must set it down just as it is, you will want to plan your changes on paper. Small value sketches will help if you wish to alter the time of day or the play of cloud shadows on a wooded hillside. Composition or format sketches will help frame your drawing to express the impact it first had on you or change it to one you wish to share with the viewer (Fig. 7-4). A vertical format may capture the drama of a waterfall or the grace of a single, slender tree. A horizontal format may help you express a broad expanse of prairie or the breathtaking chasm of the Grand Canyon.

Plan your composition. The elements of landscape can be simpli-fied to abstract forms, then restored to their wonderful complexity if you wish. One tends to think of Andrew Wyeth's work as being full of detail, but look again.

A fresh look will reveal strong abstract shapes, a bone structure on which only a few telling details may be superimposed. Thoreau's advice, ''simplify, simplify,'' can apply here as well, at least in the initial stages. Use a viewfinder to help you frame a composition and squint your eyes to help you see the strong compositional elements that first captured your eye. You may not need to change more than the superficial details to focus interest on the overall scene. In Figure 7-5 the strong sweep of the land as it becomes one with the sea carries our eye beyond the figure in the foreground to the lighthouse far in the distance. The sinuous forms of the curving shoreline have been simplified, most likely arranged by the artist to lead the eye in a smooth arc to the middle ground, then in a series of S curves to the horizon. A strong value pattern helps maintain interest and leads the viewer into the picture plane in this unusual composition. Details are secondary to the sweep of the land and the curve of the shoreline.

7-5. Notice how curved forms are used to draw the eye into the picture plane. *Port Jefferson*, by Leonid (Berman). Reproduced by permission of the Nelson-Atkins Museum of Art, Kansas City, Missouri (Nelson Fund).

7-6. This quick value and composition sketch from my field journal contains enough information to plan a painting.

7-7. Notice how value was used to explain distance and create mood in this oil. *Intimate Image #2*, by Maria Alfie. Reproduced courtesy of the artist.

overall work is quite effective. The center of interest—the trees in the middle ground and their shadows that come toward the viewer in their simplified but repeated reflections—catches and holds the viewer's eye. Even in black-and-white we can feel the calm stillness of the water and see the sunlight glinting through the back-lit trees. Background hills are treated simply, painted with a lighter value to make them recede. This painting demonstrates that a lot of detail is not necessary in effectively depicting a landscape, but a good value pattern is. (For another example of background simplification in a more complex work, see George Caleb Bingham's *Landscape with Cattle, 1846*, Fig. 5-17).

Just as effective as the more traditional broad landscape are those subjects we see every day and tend to take for granted. If *we* have done so, so have others. In our learning to see we can share what we have discovered about these ordinary scenes. An ancient grove of apple trees passed each day on the way to work may remind us of van Gogh's magnificent *The Olive Grove* (Fig. 7-8). Claude Monet immortalized a simple pond of water lilies in his *Nympheas* series, creating with his dabs and daubs of color a realer-than-real painting that calls the viewer over and over to stand bemused before its dreamlike pastels (Fig. 7-9). In Figure 7-10 Thomas Aquinas Daly, a contemporary painter, has set forth a beaver dam with the same simplicity in watercolor, making one stop and say, ''Yes, that's how it is. How could I have missed it?''

A Few Rules of Perspective

Perspective applies to landscape painting just as it does to architectural rendering. We live in time and space, and distance affects all we see. Instead of the regimented

A strong value pattern helps to define distance as well as make for a good, easily read composition (Fig. 7-6). I often use the four-value system in sketches to help simplify the landscape before me. With so many planes in the natural world, and so many values or shades of color, we need to simplify in order to understand and portray what we see.

Maria Alfie has used a scale of only four basic values to explain her subject in Figure 7-7, but the

7-8. Repeated, short, curved brush strokes convincingly depict leaves as well as give a sense of motion. *The Olive Grove*, by Vincent Van Gogh. Reproduced by permission of the Nelson-Atkins Museum of Art, Kansas City, Missouri (Nelson Fund).

lines of uprights seen in a cityscape, logically progressing away from the viewer, in landscapes we are more likely to see the effects of perspective in a line of poplars that converge as they near the vanishing point or in clouds that seem to become smaller as they near the horizon (Figs. 7-11 and 7-12). Perspective is rarely so easily detected in landscape painting, however. Whereas in a cityscape streets are often laid out in a mechanical grid, causing lines of buildings to converge according to well-defined theory, in nature the tidy grid form is quite foreign. Hills and valleys affect horizon lines and apparent if not actual vanishing points. Curves appear everywhere, in streams, tree limbs, configurations of hills. But rules of perspective, though not so readily apparent, still apply as objects advance or recede from the viewer's eye level. We need not use a T square or triangle to express this perspective, but we need to be aware of its presence. If we are seated, eye level will be low, and things above that level will appear to converge toward us at a much more acute angle than those things that fall below eye level. On the other hand, if we are perched high on the side of a hill,

7-9. A dreamlike, impressionistic painting of a lily pond. The artist used loose brushwork to express the sense of light, and color to suggest soft, summery ambience. *Nympheas*, by Claude Monet. Reproduced by permission of the Nelson-Atkins Museum of Art, Kansas City, Missouri (Nelson Fund).

7-10. This simple, affecting watercolor painting shows a beaver dam with bright streams of water spilling over it. *Wolfe Road Beaver Dam*, by Thomas Aquinas Daly. Reproduced courtesy of the artist.

7-11. Keep cloud studies in your sketchbook to remind you of perspective as well as the shapes of various cloud formations.

7-12. In this watercolor, various types of clouds (nimbostratus, cumulonimbus, and cumulus) still obey the laws of perspective, as does the landscape below. See how the artist has given a sense of distance and atmosphere to this study by using receding forms, aerial perspective, and less detail in the backround. *The Big Cloud*, by Jim Hamil. Reproduced courtesy of the artist.

things below will appear to rise at a more acute angle. Look again at Leonid's *Port Jefferson* (Fig. 7-5). Here we are led to believe we are sitting near the man on the closest dune, and everything ''below'' rises to our eye level, where it becomes much less angular and acute. Maria Alfie has used a road to convey perspective in Figure 7-13. In looking at this watercolor, you know that you are on a hill a bit below the level of the first rise in the road, perhaps sitting in the grass.

In Figure 7-14, Jacob C. Ward's painting *Natural Bridge*, we are again at a much lower level. He has used perspective in the natural bridge to give us a sense of where we are in relation to the massive landform by using shadow on the underside. We are seeing the bottom of the natural bridge as one side—the angle of the lines of the bridge itself points downward toward the center of interest. The trees on both sides of the rocky gap also follow the natural rules of perspective, as does the stream that runs underneath. Using this kind of perspective gives depth to a painting, a sense

of truth and presence. A simplified sketch helps to analyze this perspective.

Achieving a Sense of Distance

In landscape painting or drawing, distance can be indicated in a number of ways. Think again of what a camera sees; unless you have a fine lens and a perfect exposure, backgrounds probably will be much less detailed than foregrounds are. The eye sees them in this same way, and atmospheric conditions often compound this effect by blueing far hills with haze. In the midwest one often sees this haze in the morning and afternoon, or any time humidity has added moisture to the air. On a snowy or rainy day, the effect is heightened, but almost always the distance recedes visually as well as actually, becoming less detailed, more blued (Fig. 7-15). To translate what we see to the flat plane of the paper, we need simply to paint what we *see*, not what our brain tells us must be there. Trust your eyes rather than your logical mind that insists that far hill *must* be just

as tree covered, just as detailed, as the one you see nearby. Folk-art painters often use as much detail in the background as they do up close, and there is a charm to that—who can deny Grandma Moses's appeal? But unless we *are* genuinely primitive, we need to believe our eyes. Our minds often intervene, wanting us to paint green trees green and white houses white, no matter how affected by distance, haze, or reflected color they may be. The left brain with its store of knowledge has no place in this initial seeing. Later, as you put down what you observe, both brain hemispheres can work together—but first you must trust what you see. Let the right brain work.

Figure 7-16 is a good example of communicating distance. The quick sketch is the perfect place to explore this kind of simplification, since we are not temped to overwork and explain what we see. Artist Clare Walker Leslie completed this sketch of the New Hampshire hills as she rode in a car, capturing the feeling of distance by emphasizing foreground detail while simplifying distant

7-14. This painting positions the viewer with a low vanishing point. The diagram shows how this perspective is achieved. *Natural Bridge*, by Jacob C. Ward. Reproduced by permission of the Nelson-Atkins Museum of Art, Kansas City, Missouri (Nelson Fund).

forms. The mountain beyond must be as fully wooded, at least on the lower slopes, as the near hills, but our eyes do not see it so. Lines are less distinct, finer and lighter, forms are simplified, and we feel the sense of distance just as the artist did.

Two sketches from my own field journal (Fig. 7-17) suggest ways to express distance. In the first drawing, there are essentially only two planes, foreground and background, since very little was going on in between. It was a brilliantly sunny day, and the foreground trees stand out, both in detail and value, while the far hills are a single, simple shadowed form with only minimal indications of detail. They do, however, seem to recede from the viewer since they are simplified. In the second sketch, *Aug. 26, Cooley Lake*, the far lakeshore is only hinted at, pale and just barely there. Here too the background recedes, in a somewhat different way. Trust what you see, but remember to *simplify* distance, whatever value it may appear.

7-15. Notice how the artist has used a very simplified background to suggest distance. *Spring Thaw on Turkey Creek*, by Donna Aldridge. Reproduced courtesy of the artist.

Creating a sense of distance in watercolor is really quite easy and may be accomplished by several means. Either make your distances pale washes of the same color used close by adding water or opaque white, or add a bit more blue to each plane as it recedes. Some artists finish their painting completely to this stage, then add a wash of soft cobalt blue over the distant hills to give the effect of atmospheric haze. Keep these distant washes simple, cool and relatively undetailed, and they will automatically recede visually.

Man-Made Objects

Pure landscape may be enhanced by the addition of a hint of the presence of man, or even *more* than a hint if that intrusion is harmonious with your subject.

Old buildings, farmhouses, abandoned cars or bits of furniture, barns, bridges, fenceposts, fields, and other man-made additions may give an interesting tension to your work or a sense of balance (Fig. 7-18). We look for signs of human life, and where they are not to be found, we often invent them. A young artist I know finds faces and body forms in stones and trees and invites you to find them too, hidden in his intricate drawings. A village on a far hill can add to rather than detract from a rural landscape. Man-made and natural forms often work together harmoniously.

The old mineral water well in East Valley Park (Fig. 7-1) is a case in point of a man-made object fitting comfortably into a landscape. This particular drawing concentrates on the pagoda itself, but this weathered structure has appeared in my paintings and illustrations many times from a distance or as a feature in the middle ground, adding not only a sense of history and a human touch, but scale as well. The weathered stones and the twisted branches of the oak

7-16. The artist has created an illusion of distance in this pencil sketch, done while looking out a car window. Notice the simplification of forms and lighter values in the background. *Winchendon, N.H. 2-2-84,* by Clare Walker Leslie. Reproduced courtesy of the artist.

Siloam Mountain Park
long way around!

Aug. 26, Cooley Lake

7-17. Visual distance is hinted at in these two field sketches. Notice how the two techniques are really quite different but still manage to make the background recede. In the first, the light, more highly detailed foreground tree stands out against a simple, dark background. The second sketch uses the perspective of the road to suggest distance.

complement each other, and one without the other would not be as interesting.

Intimate Landscapes

While the word *landscape* conjures up a vision of broad vistas, wide-open spaces, a larger-than-life world encountered from a high vantage point or a spectacular overlook, an *intimate* landscape is somehow more approachable, more comfortable, more accessible. It is not necessary to go to great lengths to find something spectacular to render—intimate landscapes are everywhere, just outside your door and hidden in the deepest forest (Fig. 7-19). These small serendipities sometimes have more power to touch

7-18. This late-fall watercolor is enhanced by the hint of man's presence in the old gate. Drawing or
painting nature need not preclude
evidence of man's occupancy of the
land—including this evidence sets
up a visual tension that invites par-
ticipation by the viewer. *The Gate*,
by Jim Hamil. Reproduced courtesy
of the artist and Farmland Industries.

us than the magnificent but sometimes overpowering scenes we
travel miles to find (Fig. 7-20). A
turn of a stream, gurgling com-
panionably over rocks; an ancient
weathered stump; the way light
plays across a snow-bedecked
thorny trunk; a leaf caught in a
frozen puddle; a beaver's lodge—
these things catch at our hearts,
carrying more meaning than we
realize (Fig. 7-21). Perhaps the
view outside our own window attracts us, as it did Charles Reid in
his painting *Deck Chair* (Fig. 7-22).
Our eye is drawn beyond the chair
to the quiet cove, painted simply
with few strokes but captured perfectly nonetheless. We do not
need to search the far horizons for
subjects; we need only to become
more intimate with the ones we
see every day and give them the
respect and attention they deserve
(Fig. 7-23). It is a Zen discipline to
become aware of what is—what
simply is—before us. In painting
what is, we become aware of its
eternal significance (Fig. 7-24).

7-19. The frosty broken panes of my old
cold frame, choked with weeds, caught
my eye in this intimate landscape, found
outside my back door. *The Cold Frame*,
by Cathy Johnson. Reproduced courtesy
of *The Artist's Magazine*.

7-20. This artist has found what might be
called an intimate seascape on the beach
near her Florida home. Textures of the
various shells provide a fascinating composition in this colored-pencil drawing.
Mixed Company, by Mathilde Duffy.
Reproduced courtesy of the artist.

7-21. The complexities of a beaver's lodge were explored in this intimate landscape done on toned paper with felt-tipped pens and white Prismacolor pencil. *Watkins Mill Beavers*, by Cathy Johnson.

7-22. Even the view from a window can enclose an intimate landscape, as this oil painting demonstrates. *Deck Chair*, by Charles Reid. Reproduced courtesy of the artist.

7-23. This weathered stump was found not in a forest but at the edge of a downtown Kansas City parking lot. *Weathered*, by Cathy Johnson.

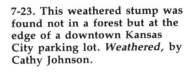

7-24. The Chinese artist Li K'an was a master at depicting the Zen-like simplicity of what is. This painting was no doubt done on rice paper, using traditional calligraphic brush strokes. Experiment with the Oriental style to achieve a new simplicity in your own work. *Ink Bamboo*, by Li K'an. Reproduced by permission of the Nelson-Atkins Museum of Art, Kansas City, Missouri (Nelson Fund).

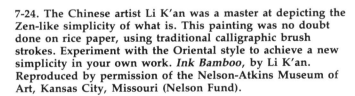

that the world is indeed round: if external forces have anything to say about it, wind and erosion will render our earth a perfect sphere. Internal forces, of course, work at cross-purposes, throwing up great shards of earth or forming sinkholes, forms also affected and explained visually with light and shade.

When expressing these shadows in watercolor, keep a container of clear water nearby to alter intensity or soften edges. Some shadows, of course, are the same value throughout, especially if they are short and close to the object itself. Others, as they fall away, pale almost to invisibility. Earth forms have softer shadowed edges as they turn toward the light, unless they are jagged rocks in strong sunlight. Soften shadow edges with clear water or a damp tissue. Light and shade and colors reflected back into shadows give life to your work, a sense of reality and presence (Figs. 7-27 and 7-28).

7-26. Cloud shadows and the softly shaded banks of hills in this oil by landscape master Asher B. Durand exhibit the subtleties of the art of using light and shadow. Look closely to see where the land masses are shaded by clouds and where they are shaped by cast shadows. *Landscape*, by Asher B. Durand. Reproduced by permission of the Nelson-Atkins Museum of Art, Kansas City, Missouri (Nelson Fund).

Frederick Franck expresses this well in his books on seeing, drawing, and Zen. Look into Franck's works as a rich source for a growing appreciation of life as it is, and you will never want for suitable subjects again.

Light and Shadow

In landscapes as in other forms of art, light and shadow help to de-

fine shapes and explain forms. Shadows help show planes and provide definition for large forms. They aid in explaining perspective and direction, as in Ward's *Natural Bridge* (see Fig. 7-14). Clouds massing in a clear blue sky affect the earth below as they cast moving shadows over the land (Fig. 7-25). The shadowed sides of the landforms themselves, like those in Figure 7-26, help us to realize

Abstraction and Realism

People often think that landscape painting must be abstract or realistic, one or the other—and preferably the latter. Nothing could be farther from the truth. All good art has its foundation in abstraction, whether we realize it or not, whether that is our primary intention or not. Abstraction may be a simplification of form for composition's sake, a strong foundation for a more realistic work (Fig. 7-29). Or the abstraction may be the final form taken by the work of art. Neither is more or less valid than the other—it depends on

7-27. Reflections can also convey the action of light in our works. See how the artist has used the simplified reflections in this farm pond to give a feeling of calm, limpid water. *Farm Pond*, by Keith Hammer. Reproduced courtesy of the artist.

7-28. Light and shadow were masterfully used to show the rough-and-tumble character of the snowy gorge in this pastel. Notice the directional character of the strokes as well. *January Wilderness*, by Donna Aldridge. Reproduced courtesy of the artist.

7-29. The artist has simplified and abstracted forms in this watercolor of mud flats by a river. Even though the painting itself is not abstract, it shows how individual forms may be symbolized with very simple, direct strokes. A strong value pattern forms the base upon which this work is built. *Kaw River Sunset*, by Jim Hamil. Reproduced courtesy of the artist.

what *you* want to say and what *you* see. Georgia O'Keeffe's wonderful paintings are realistic abstractions, that is, realistic objects used in a strongly abstract way. They are clean and powerful— nothing sweetly sentimental here, but symbolic, mystical, otherworldly.

All art rests on what might be called an abstract base, the framework of a composition. A beautiful painting or drawing will still be beautiful even if reduced to its abstract forms.

Abstractionism may be used to capture the essence of a place or time, a feeling rather than a carefully spelled out or scientifically delineated subject. You may be able to eliminate what you *see* in order to reveal what you *feel* and thereby capture the spirit of nature more fully. Figure 7-30 conveys the sense of an organic mass, what I call an intimate landscape, without a single recognizable object. It captures the essence of a muddy pool full of plant matter or landforms at the edge of a tide

pool much better than an overworked realistic drawing might, and can carry whatever imaginings we bring to it by not being too specific.

Other artists abstract nature in a more stylistic way. Repeated forms, strong evocative colors, simplified shapes, all express this kind of abstraction. J. L. McKeehan's *Gathering* (see Fig. 5-13) shows how natural forms might be transmuted into strong, abstract patterns capable of expressing a truth about nature.

CHAPTER EIGHT

All Creatures Great and Small

8-1

One of the most interesting and challenging aspects of drawing or painting from nature is that of capturing the beauty, life, and presence of animals, not only the majestic elk or the ingratiating chickadee, but the wealth of sea and pond life, the amphibians and reptiles, the fascinating insects (Fig. 8-2). The beauty and variety of these life forms, so different from our own in habitat and life-style, humbles as it amazes. These creatures are a part of the natural world in a way we have long since forgotten, but by their very presence they stir vague longings, almost a nostalgia for the simplicity of a life lived without our psychological and economic pressures. As we be-

come more intimately acquainted with these creatures we hope to capture on paper or canvas, we may be disabused of some romantic notions—the food chain is very evident at this level, and the predator/prey relationship is almost constantly before us (Fig. 8-3). This does not mean we lose the sense of beauty—or even our own vague longing. Because we are able to see life as it *is* and not as we might dream, we may bring a new power to our world. Look at the art of Glen Loates, for instance (see Bibliography). In many of his paintings, this adversarial relationship is very evident, but it in no way detracts from the beauty of his work. Other artists prefer to concentrate on animals in more

offhand and relaxed attitudes. The big cats, for instance, spend only a tiny percentage of their time at the kill; mostly they just loaf, and very elegantly at that. The herbivores make fascinating subjects, from the tiny, brilliant ruby-throated hummingbird to the wonderfully indolent hippo.

It has been said before, but it bears repeating: *nothing* beats time spent in the field, actually observing the animals, whether in their natural habitat or in a wildlife preserve or zoo (Fig. 8-4). Your sketches are invaluable as learning tools. Only a few quick lines of a gesture drawing may tell you volumes about an animal's posture, habitat, life. A stiffly posed but perfectly executed finished

93

8-2. These studies of flies capture some of the fascinating variety of insect life. Pencil drawing, by Ann Zwinger. Reproduced courtesy of the artist. From *A Desert Country Near the Sea*, 1983, published by Harper and Row.

8-3. This study of a red-tailed hawk shows its perfectly adapted food-gathering appendages in detail. *Red-tailed Hawk*, by Cathy Johnson. Reproduced courtesy of the Martha Lafite Thompson Nature Sanctuary.

turn; wait for that characteristic stretch, prowl, or turn and you can catch it.

If your subject *does* fly or run, however, repeated action drawing will be of no use. In this case you must train your eye to *see* what you are looking at—let it become a part of you, even if for only that split second before your subject flies off (Fig. 8-6). Have you ever noticed how, in looking for a particular passage in a book, you can often remember on what side of the opened book it was, approximately where on the page? In a bit the same way, you can envision what you have seen and put it on paper. You have heard the phrase ''your mind's eye''—use that phenomenon to convey on paper the ephemeral quality of a bird's flight. See, first in your mind and then on your paper, how that heron's legs were outstretched in flight, how his neck curved back on itself as he flew overhead; the incredible wingspan. Visualize those spacial relationships and sketch them quickly onto your paper. Of course, you will not create a detailed nature study complete enough to use in a field guide. But you *will* create a true reflection of an instant in time.

Wildlife Art: From the General to the Particular

We have looked at wildlife art in a general way so far. But we do

piece will not have half the vitality of these quick, accurate studies done on the spot. Use them as bases for your drawings, *then* go ahead and draw every feather if you wish.

Birds and other wildlife move, and move fast. They will not hold still and pose for you unless they are totally unaware of your presence or you are lucky enough to catch them sleeping. If you want a pose that suggests all the grace and beauty of animals in action, you have to be prepared to work quickly and to look at the creatures in a new way (Fig. 8-5). Attune yourself to their motion. If you are lucky, you will not scare the animal away, only catch it in a repeated or cyclical action. The pose you are interested in will re-

8-4. This pencil study of ring-tailed lemurs was done at the zoo. *Ring-tailed Lemurs*, by Cathy Johnson.

8-5. These sketches of my cat at his bath time were done quickly as he shifted from pose to pose. This same technique can be used with any rapidly moving animal.

8-6. These pencil studies are basically silhouettes, completed from memory after the sparrows flew away. *Sparrows*, by Cathy Johnson.

not paint birds or mammals; we paint a *particular* bird—a hawk or sparrow or chickadee—a *particular* mammal—a bear or moose or squirrel. Unless you are drawing a fantastic creature from your own imagination, you will be looking at *some* particular subject, whether live, in a museum diorama, or in a photograph. (And even if you are working from your imagination, that very particular beast has special and individual characteristics in your mind's eye.) Whenever you touch pencil to paper, you necessarily leave the general behind in a quest for the particular.

Each animal has a characteristic stance, mood, or aura that you can capture in your drawings to give them a sense of life (Fig. 8-7). Unless you are working from a poorly stuffed specimen, this sense of life gives authenticity to your work (Fig. 8-8). A reasonable acquaintance with your subject will help you focus on what these characteristic poses and actions are. *One* photo, *one* resource will not suffice: by relying on only one source, you will be caught up in copying what is essentially only a singular flat image.

Getting inside Your Subject

Much has been said about *literally* getting inside an animal in order to understand how it moves, strikes poses, flies, and performs its other activities. A good book on anatomy is invaluable for this type of study, although being able to find the *particular* skeletal forma-

tion for your *particular* creature is not quite as important as understanding how that creature's *family* works. If you understand how the skeleton of a horse, cat, dog, or deer works—how the hip bones swivel from the pelvis, how the long bones of the leg fit together, how the foot corresponds to or differs from our own—you will be able to manipulate poses of any of these (or related) species with some degree of authority. An

8-7. This wonderful pencil, watercolor, and gouache drawing is of a very particular boar indeed. The artist has captured the facial expression and stance with much personality. *A Boar*, by Sir Edwin Landseer. Reproduced by permission of the Nelson-Atkins Museum of Art, Kansas City, Missouri (Nelson Fund).

8-8. The artist has used colored pencils in this lifelike drawing of a red fox. Notice how she used individual pencil strokes to capture the softness of the fox's fur. The mood here is one of alert watchfulness. *Red Fox*, by Carol Sorensen. Reproduced courtesy of the artist.

understanding of the skeleton of one kind of bird will help you understand the workings of another. Granted, the differences between the flightless penguin and the elegantly soaring hawk stretch the point a bit, but a basic understanding will see you through a great many situations.

The same principle applies to the musculature or fleshiness of an animal. A basic understanding of the large muscle groups of a family will help you translate information from one species to another without having to cultivate an almost medical knowledge of the names and functions of the muscles of a particular animal. If such information is available, it will be helpful to you. If not, your own observations and instincts are always with you—trust them.

Perhaps as important as *literally* getting inside your subject is the ability to relate psychologically, to understand with your heart (and instincts) what makes an animal tick. Clare Walker Leslie says that it is necessary to draw and redraw a chickadee many times to understand what makes it uniquely and recognizably a chickadee and finds this an important concept in her art (Fig. 8-9).

Those hours of observation and your own field sketches will pay off in understanding, in a kind of almost mystical rapport with your subject that will allow you to depict it in whatever pose, whatever situation (Fig. 8-10). Do not be discouraged by this emphasis on hours spent on drawing and redrawing an animal. Nothing comes without work, nothing sticks with us until it becomes a part of us. (And nothing is more enjoyable than these hours spent in the field, sketchbook in hand. Nature is a wonderful teacher; patient, beautiful, always available, challenging—and free.)

8-9. This sketchbook page is filled with quick studies of a chickadee. Drawings like this help us to understand our subjects, get inside them. Sketchbook page, by Clare Walker Leslie. Reproduced courtesy of the artist.

Household Pets Make Handy Models

In winter, at night, when it is pouring rain, when you are ill, or any time you simply want to keep your hand in and stay in practice, your pet may be your best model (Fig. 8-11). If you gain an understanding of how your cat works, sketch it washing, playing, or loafing, you have a working knowledge of the feline, from bobcats to cougars. The family dog will stand in for coyotes, wolves, and foxes in his basic form as well as his stance when eating, running, or sleeping. Yorkies, alas, are not quite as useful for this purpose as the sleeker, more muscular hounds or the wolf-like huskies, but even these lovable mops will help you understand the canine's paw construction, eyes, nose, and other features. If you are lucky enough to have an aquarium of tropical fish, you will have many shapes, behavior patterns, and scale configurations to choose from. A goldfish might, for instance, stand in for a carp (Fig. 8-12).

Practice with quick contour drawings, gesture sketches, detail studies, or complete drawings of the animals at hand. Try different techniques, different ways of handling your pencil or brush. Do a page of eye studies or ears or paws or noses, from all angles (Fig. 8-13). The understanding

8-10. In this painting, the artist has gotten inside his subject psychologically and symbolically, proving it is not necessary to do a realistic, feather-by-feather rendering to produce a terrific piece of art. *Magpie Talisman*, by John Stewart. Reproduced courtesy of the artist.

Alice, sleeping
(aerial veiw)

8-11. My cat "posing," unaware. *Alice*, by Cathy Johnson.

8-12. These beautiful carp may have been the pets of the Chinese artist. Notice the stylized beauty of their scale patterns and the repeated motif of waves. *Carp*, by Ho K'o-Ch'ang. Reproduced by permission of the Nelson-Atkins Museum of Art, Kansas City, Missouri.

8-13. A page of eye studies such as this helps me to draw details with authority in a more finished piece. Sketchbook page, by Cathy Johnson. Reproduced courtesy of *The Artist's Magazine*.

M'Gow and her eye

P-Port's Profile

Alice's Eye

8-14. This scientific illustration of a snail has been beautifully rendered in pencil. Subtle tonal variations are used to express the spiraling shell. *Helix aspersa*, by Pattie L. Paris. Reproduced courtesy of the artist.

8-15. Use of a bird feeder allowed me to get close enough to this little fellow to do a creditable rendering as part of a Christmas card design. *Tufted Titmouse*, by Cathy Johnson.

8-17. This field sketch has captured the stern upright posture of the great horned owl. Notice how its center of gravity is a vertical line. *Great Horned Owl*, by Clare Walker Leslie. Reproduced courtesy of the artist.

you gain of animal anatomy and perspective will come into play all your working life.

Household *non*-pets (generally considered to be pests instead) make interesting models as well. A daddy long-legs became a part of Figure 4-7 when he took up residence on my philodendron. Pill bugs occasionally find their way into the best of homes, as do crickets, spiders, flies, ants, and roaches. With the exception of the last, I have enjoyed drawing the creatures I share my home with. A fear of spiders disappeared when I began to look at them with an artist's eye. We can learn a lot from the way a cricket's legs join and bend like a suit of armor, or from the delightful armadillolike pill bug. Houseflies may disgust you, but they make good models.

8-16. This drawing provides a peek into the life of these mallard chicks. Litho pencil was used to render the soft downy feathers of the young ducklings. *New Mallards*, by Ernest Lussier. Reproduced courtesy of the artist.

In an older home you may even play host to an occasional snail in the basement; these are as beautiful to draw as their marine counterparts (Fig. 8-14).

Birds

Birds have fascinated us for centuries. We have toyed with the idea of flight and studied these feathered flyers in hopes of learning their secrets. We have built ourselves wooden wings and covered them with feathers, trying to soar. We envy these lovely, free creatures, and we capture them in art if not in reality. Roger Tory Peterson, Louis Agassiz Fuertes, John James Audubon, Charles Tunnicliffe—the names of accomplished and beloved painters of birds are often household words. These airborne creatures are the

8-19. The angle of a bird's stance will change, of course, depending on where it is in relation to your paper and whether it is sitting quietly, feeding, or about to take off. A quick angle line will help you establish the basic posture. Ovals for body and head and geometric shapes for the wings, tail, and beak will help simplify the overall shape.

8-18. Compare the feeding stance of the Canada geese here with the stance of the owl in Fig. 8-17. *Canadas at Winter Cornfield*, by Jan Martin McGuire. Reproduced courtesy of the artist.

most frustrating subjects—they are quick, they are skittish, and all summer they seem to be only gray shadows flitting tantalizingly through the dense leaves. A pair of binoculars or a spotting scope is a great help to the serious bird painter, as is a simple bird feeder for the more urbanized species (Fig. 8-15). Chickadees, juncos, titmice, cardinals, jays, ruby-crowned kinglets, even wood-

peckers and crows may frequent your feeder, giving you excellent opportunities to sketch. Hawks, owls, ravens, eagles, pheasants, whippoorwills, and quail are not as accustomed to humans, and stalking them with the idea of "bringing them back alive" on your paper or canvas is a real challenge (Fig. 8-16). A scope, a camera with a telephoto lens, stuffed specimens, or study skins may be

necessary to help capture details unless you are able to spend many hours in a blind. Be careful when working from a stuffed bird, however. *Know* your subject, its configuration and stance, before relying on the taxidermist's art for feathers, claws, and other details. I once did a painting I was quite proud of, a watercolor of a hawk. Unfortunately, *both* the taxidermist and I were amateurs, and the

8-20. This baby screech owl was found at the local golf course. I kept it safe until it could be released to its parents the following night. Such a captive subject makes it easier to explore body shape, feather placement, stance, and details such as eyes, beaks, and feet. *Owlet*, by Cathy Johnson.

8-21. The artist has carefully placed a highlight in this little fellow's eye to give a sense of life in this brush-and-ink drawing. *Wood Rat*, by Charles W. Schwartz. Reproduced courtesy of the artist, the Conservation Commission of the State of Missouri, and the Missouri Historical Society.

bird's stance was much too horizontal, his legs much too far back for reality. If you are sure the bird (or animal) has been correctly mounted, then of course this will allow you to sketch it at a number of angles, becoming much more intimate with perspective than you would be able to in the field or when working from photographs. Be aware that the color of a mounted specimen or study skin will fade with age, though.

Stance, or attitude, in a bird is most important and should be studied closely (Figs. 8-17 and 8-18). Does it sit upright, at an angle, or horizontally? Where does its center of gravity lie? Indicate the line formed by the basic body attitude first, and hang your whole drawing from that angle (Fig. 8-19). A nuthatch works its way head first down a tree, while a downy woodpecker may pass going in the opposite direction. A painting of a nuthatch "swimming upstream" is going to look odd, even though it may occasionally head in that direction.

Study the various beak shapes. Is your subject's beak heavy, stubby, and bold? Your bird probably needs this nutcrackerlike appendage to crack seeds. A robin is well equipped to probe the soil for earthworms: its beak is long and slender. An eagle or hawk has a hooked beak, well suited to rending the flesh that makes up a predator's diet (see Fig. 8-3). Careful observation will help you to make an accurate drawing.

Look for other body characteristics as well: wingspan and wing shape, depth of the bird's chest (remember those busty pigeons!), configuration of the feet, shape of the tail. All of these anatomical details will help you to render a believable bird once you have settled on its basic body shape and stance.

Many artists use a series of ovals to draw the basic shape. If it helps you to draw an accurate bird, try

8-22. These are only a few of the ways to render hair or fur. Different media will require different methods. Experiment to find your own, and try to analyze how some of the artists in this book have dealt with the problem.

this: first, draw the angle of its stance, lightly, on your paper. With quick gestures, draw the large oval body, and the smaller oval head, paying attention to the length of the neck (if one is visible at all) and the angle the head is held at, as well as the negative spaces that surround these details (see Fig. 8-19). Add the characteristic beak shape, carefully relating it to the angle of the head; then draw in the eyes, crown, wings, tail, legs, and feet. You may then take detail as far as you like.

Any good field guide to the birds will tell you how your bird

is feathered. Wings have primary as well as secondary feathers, wing coverts, and scapulars. Wing shape as well as configuration vary with the particular bird.

Some artists study birds for a lifetime and make them their primary or only subject, and for such artists this information will only provide a beginning. Firsthand observation and years of practice will fill in the gaps (Fig. 8-20).

Mammals
Mammals are particularly attractive subjects for drawing and painting. These warm-blooded

a   b

8-23. The spine of a mammal forms its posture line. You can convey a feeling of life and motion if you perceive it correctly. As with bird drawings (see Fig. 8-19), this cat was seen first as a series of ovals for body, shoulders, and head. If breaking down an animal's shape into such components helps you to see what is before you, try this exercise.

creatures seem more closely related to ourselves, and so they are—we all belong to the same class, Mammalia.

Many mammals are appealing, with soft fur, bottomless eyes, and easy grace. But those very features make them a real challenge to draw. Eyes must look lively: if animals have a soul—and I feel they must—it shines from those eyes (Fig. 8-21). Fur is endlessly tricky to render; unless the basic form is right, no amount of careful detailing of individual hairs is going to help. How far *do* you

need to go to represent fur? How much detail makes you happy? Glen Loates and Nicholas Wilson paint virtually every hair, and beautifully. Bob Kuhn and Fred Machetanz do not—and consider the samples of various ways to render fur in Figure 8-22, and try them out. Try your own and see what suits your needs.

Look for overall directional lines to capture a pose; the spine is often quite expressive. In Figure 8-23a I looked for the angle and shape of the line to suggest a sitting and lying cat.

Simplifying body shapes may help to capture pose as well as body configuration, as in Figure 8-23b; you can see that I used a series of ovals to define the cat's form in the preliminary drawing, then fleshed out the drawing in the final stage.

It is interesting to show mammals in their natural habitat, going about their private lives, as Figure 8-24 does. These views have a power to touch that the necessarily diagnostic studies in field guides might not. Anatomical pose is of primary importance,

8-24. This litho-pencil drawing shows a young buck in his natural habitat. *Sneaking Out*, by Ernest Lussier. Reproduced courtesy of the artist.

but the details of habitat and season add immeasurably to our ability to understand and relate to the subject (Fig. 8-25).

Again, animals in the wild, in zoos, or in wildlife preserves offer the best opportunities for study and sketching (Fig. 8-26). Mounted specimens never look quite the same, since the gloss leaves the fur and the eyes soon after death—even coloration is different. Glass eyes are quite good these days, but they can never fix you with the chilling stare or melting glance a live animal can give you.

Museum mounts may be the best available stuffed specimens. Those in dioramas offer the opportunity to study habitat and possibly other species that occupy the same slice of country. You may be able to position yourself to draw the animal from several angles to get a better understanding of its anatomy (Fig. 8-27). Lighting here is often poor, however, in order to preserve the specimens

8-25. This moose is in its natural feeding element, water. Watercolor study, by Cathy Johnson.

without fading, and you may have trouble discerning details.

Fish

Graceful and secret shapes in a milieu alien to humans, fish have symbolized many things in many cultures. Their sinuous grace and wonderful coloration make them a joy to draw and paint (Fig. 8-28). As design forms, they are unequaled. Their shapes are deceptively simple—an oval with a tail might seem to describe them—but their swift turns and

8-26. This pencil drawing of a prong-horn was refined as I went along. Wrong lines were allowed to stand without erasing, and new lines were simply added in the correct position. When working from life, often there is not time to erase and perfect as you go.

8-27. The raccoon in this diorama at the Kansas City Museum of History and Science was positioned close to the glass so I could draw its defensive posture from several angles.

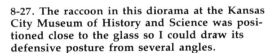

8-28. This drawing captures the power of the big fish in its element. *Jumping Free*, by Ernest Lussier. Reproduced courtesy of the artist.

8-29. The eyes have a hazy softness of youth in this pencil drawing of a young owl. *Barred Owl*, by Charles W. Schwartz. Reproduced courtesy of the artist, the Conservation Commission of the State of Missouri, and the University of Missouri Press.

moves give these underwater creatures a dynamism challenging to try to capture. Mouths, eye placement, gills, fins, and tail shapes need to be carefully observed, but fish are all—literally—streamlining. Capture that and you have got the essence. Often in drawing animals, I begin with the eyes, not a very scientific or systematic beginning, I admit, but I go for the sense of life (Fig. 8-29). I may do a quick rough of the basic outline first, just to get the shape or stance right, but then I try for the eyes. When they are right, the rest of the composition can follow. If they are wrong, it is best to throw out the whole thing and start over. We see with our eyes, and we interact with other species through these organs as well. If your work has a kind of life that draws the viewer's eye, strikes a response, then it is worth pursuing. It is not necessary to portray all your subjects with direct eye contact, of course. Although a frontal stare can be affecting, the basic shyness of some animals can be expressed through averted eyes or lowered lids.

CHAPTER NINE

Keeping a Field Sketchbook

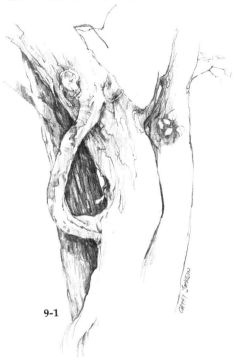

9-1

The Field Sketchbook as Diary

A field sketchbook is an invaluable tool for those who will use their observations in later works, for those who wish to study and learn from nature; for biologists, ecologists, botanists, and other scientists; and for those who simply enjoy recording life and experiences. Mine has become more of a naturalist's journal than a sketchbook, a record of my rambles along the banks of the Fishing River and through the old-growth forest that crowns nearby Siloam Mountain. Many people have found similar uses for their field sketchbooks: valuable records of trips to places far and near, learning tools, a way of revisiting, almost reexperiencing, special times and places (Fig. 9-2).

What is a diary but a book of days, a place to record your thoughts, feelings, experiences? When your days—or a part of them at any rate—are spent in nature, whether in your own backyard or at the top of a mountain, you have a special kind of experience to record. As an artist, your natural environment can be a constant source of wonder, of inspiration, of discovery. Your time here is precious, not only as means to an end—the creative production of a drawing, a painting, or an illustration—but as an end in itself.

My own field sketchbook has changed over time, metamorphosed into a series of vignetted days caught forever like flies in amber (Fig. 9-3). It stands or falls on its own. Its pages may be *interspersed* with value sketches, studies, or drawings intended as research for something else, but the journal itself has become a book of my discovery of my life, my self, my relationship to nature. These pages, with their quick drawings and penciled notes, are always there to return to on a winter day to find spring, on sad days to find joy, on cloud-filled days to find sun.

As an artist, you may find your best friend is your sketchbook. When you are unable to take the time to paint, or when you cannot carry the necessary equipment into the field for a detailed watercolor study; when that incredible,

Common Blue - tiny

bid brown skipper on a grape leaf

yellow center

Blue Damsel-fly -

Common Sunflower

light green, hairy stem 3' tall

July 24, '84

a cuckoo watches while I draw

tiny, metallic green bees collect pollen

cool this morning

river dribbles over the rocks — it's very low

frogs mostly quiet this a.m.

owl hoots on the hill - still up (probably Barred Owl)

Smell of sun on grasses — clover — grape flowers this late?

Birds are all bathing or drinking - fly up as I walk along the bank

brownish brown

satiny green

Squirrel-chewed? acorn

reddish bu

ck! ck! ck! ck! weeow

spotted, grayish brown darker tail - about 8" long - scoll - up but doesn't fly - though I'm only 10' away — Just nearby?

Juvenile Wood Thrush?

July 27, '84

Ancient Picnic Spot, East Valley Park

remains of a stone-based table, a crumbling bench — it reminds me of Stonehenge. Only robins, crows, Eastern wood phoebes, juncos & chickadees picnic here now — and the occasional rabbit.

A young heron flew up off the creek Brown thrasher in the woods edge

9-2 and 9-3. Field sketchbook pages and notes.

fully opened blood root - April 26

most of the others have lost their petals

Cadmium yellow centers

9-4. This sketch was done with an HB woodless drawing pencil from Progresso. The bloodroot flowers had popped up all over the woods when I happened across them in April.

huge turkey vulture rises flapping from the roadside to land on a fencepost only a few feet away; when the sun breaks through the clouds after days of overcast, giving new meaning to the phrase ''silver lining''; when you are riding along in the car and a sudden vista drops away between two Ozark ridges—that is the time to grab your sketchbook. You may be too rushed to take the time for a painting—or even a detailed study—but those quick field sketches and a few notes will be enough to recall the excitement later.

You may want to use your sketchbook to plan future works, to try out compositions or format studies, to do detail studies—to explore and to learn.

I once spent a long afternoon waiting for my car to be repaired, but rather than being bored or watching the dealer's television set, I used the time to study the pigeons on nearby rooftops and sidewalks in my sketchbook. Before, birds had simply been bent lines in the skies of my landscapes, but the next painting I did of an ancient city building was brought to life by a descending flock of pigeons casting their angular shadows on the warm brick wall.

My sketchbook has become a repository of moments and days like this, an invaluable tool (Figs. 9-4 and 9-5). You can use yours to record these instants in time, to plan future works, to record unusual flowers or plants you come across in your rambles, to study nature's evolutionary designs, or

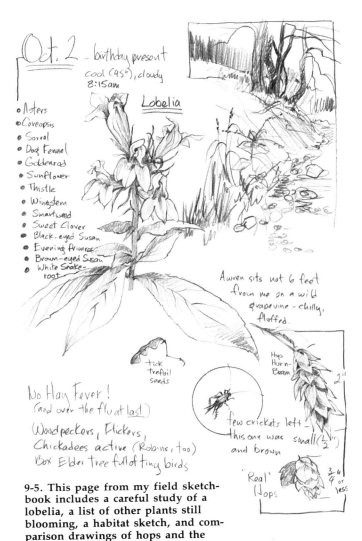

9-5. This page from my field sketchbook includes a careful study of a lobelia, a list of other plants still blooming, a habitat sketch, and comparison drawings of hops and the fruit of a hop hornbeam tree—plus a celebration of the end of hay fever!

9-6. Field sketches, by Gordon Morrison, from the *Curious Naturalist*, published by Prentice-Hall, Inc. Reproduced courtesy of the artist and Prentice-Hall, Inc.

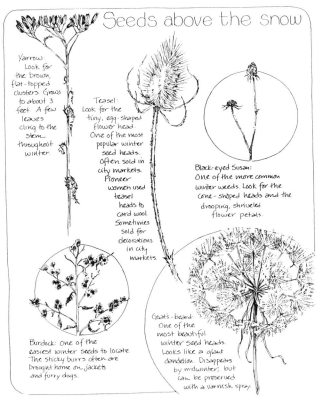

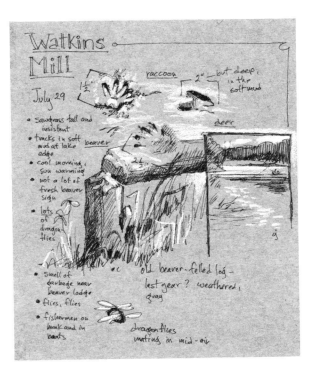

9-7. Field sketch from Watkins Mill, done with felt-tipped pen and white Prismacolor pencil on tan paper.

to make quick habitat sketches. It is an antidote to boredom, a passport to learning, a place to dream.

Most artists I have talked to guard their field notes jealously. Many graciously shared their pages for this book, but most preferred to send reproductions of journal pages rather than interrupt the continuity of what becomes a very personal record of observations and events (Fig. 9-6). I too was reluctant to tear days out of my *own* book, because the orderly progression of days well spent is comforting to look back on in times when deadlines press, the phone jangles constantly, and

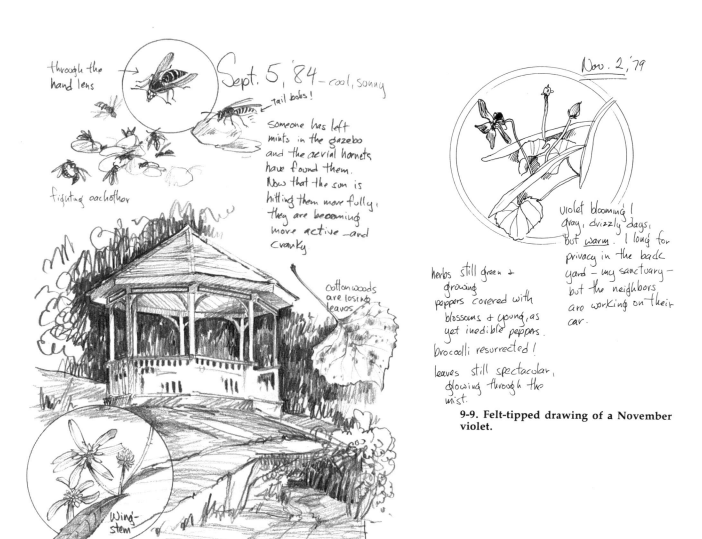

through the hand lens

Sept. 5, '84 — cool, sunny

Tail bobs!

Someone has left mints in the gazebo and the aerial hornets have found them. Now that the sun is hitting them more fully, they are becoming more active — and cranky

fighting eachother

cotton woods are losing leaves

Wing-stem

CAT

Nov. 2, '79

violet blooming! gray, drizzly days, but warm. I long for privacy in the back yard — my sanctuary — but the neighbors are working on their car.

herbs still green & growing
peppers covered with blossoms & young, as yet inedible peppers.
broccoli resurrected!
leaves still spectacular, glowing through the mist.

9-9. Felt-tipped drawing of a November violet.

9-8. Studies of aerial hornets and wing-stem. Such drawings help fix names and dates in mind.

demands for my time and attention make me feel as if my edges were beginning to fray and tatter.

Robert Bateman uses his sketchbook to record his travels, a visual record of far places and new sights (and sounds—penciled notes add a lot). Sketching is a much more interesting, involving, and immediate way for an artist to record these experiences than photography is. A camera may record only what is there, but often you must wait until after the film is developed and prints are made to see if you captured the image you sought. If you discover you did not, it is often too late. A quick, personal sketch of just what you are witnessing surely preserves just the images you want to record (Fig. 9-7).

I also find that my journal is important in recording events I might forget and for learning the shapes and names of flowers, plants, and insects in a way that helps me interact with my subjects on a much more intimate level than simply looking up the facts in a field guide. These researched facts are like quicksilver to me, almost as easily forgotten as they were ''learned.'' My jottings and sketches in a field journal, however, take my time and attention, fully if briefly (Fig. 9-8). That bug or bud or branch becomes a friend, one I will recall. Remember visual aids in school? Our own visual aids stay with us just that much longer.

How often do we see an unusual (if tiny) event that catches our attention, touches us in a special way, only to forget it later? If we record these happenings in a sketchbook, we can recapture these moments over and over. Not only is it interesting and useful to recall just which late fall day we found a violet in full bloom or saw a sun dog in a summer sky, but we can remember through these pages the circumstances and events that surrounded that moment (Fig. 9-9). A once-in-a-

9-10. Pencil drawing of two pelicans done while in Florida on a sketching trip. *Pelicans*, by Sharon Stolzenberger. Reproduced courtesy of the artist.

9-11. This sketch captures a fox as it snoozes on its den site. Sketchbook page, by Clare Walker Leslie. Reproduced courtesy of the artist.

lifetime trip to the moors of Scotland or the swamps of Florida can be relived again and again (Fig. 9-10). A photo, of course, will serve to remind us visually. Emotionally, spiritually, our own sketches—however rough or quickly done—will ''bring it back alive.''

Field Notes

In an artist's sketchbook you will find mostly thumbnail sketches, value studies, drawings (Fig. 9-11), plus perhaps a close-up or detail of the subject, with color notes. The notes in a naturalist's sketchbook may include all of that and a good deal more. Subjects of interest to the naturalist are not only visual but aural and olfactory as well. What do you hear? Bird calls? What kind? Where? How often? In what season? What smells are there? Flowers, dead leaves, mushrooms? Perhaps a stinkhorn or a skunk? I often list the birds I see on a particular day as well as sketching any that are close

enough. To aid in identification, I make notes as to their calls, where and when they gave them, what they were doing at the time (courting, nesting, defending territory?). I may add color notes or information about special markings to my rough sketches.

Once a week or so, I list flowers I have seen to become familiar with their names and the season in which they grow. In early October an elderly gentleman I met on the path remarked that the flowers were almost gone. The day before I had listed twenty-eight species on that same stretch of path! I also note color variations (often the same flower is brighter in full sun than in shade) and draw a flower carefully for identification if I do not know its name. One autumn day I simply listed all the color nuances I saw and was amazed at how many and varied they were once I began naming them. Fall is not just red and orange and yellow!

Date, meteorological conditions, time of day, plus any odd sounds

or sights may complete my field notes (Fig. 9-12). If I do not have time to draw a bird as it flashes by or a groundhog as it scuttles away, at least I can do a quick gesture sketch and note as much pertinent information as I can remember, while it is fresh. These field notes are excellent guides for later study, useful for anyone in the outdoor sciences as well as a wildlife artist or illustrator.

Often on my walks I spend thirty minutes to two hours rambling, sketching, taking notes. When I get home, I can get out my field guides and identify species, look up folklore or specific uses for herbs or flowers, and add any clarifying information to my sketchbook page. This may take two minutes or a half hour, but it is well worth the time. In effect, I am writing my own field guide to my home area. You can do the same, not only as an invaluable aid in adding depth, believability, and atmosphere to your work, but as a way to become a part of your specific habitat.

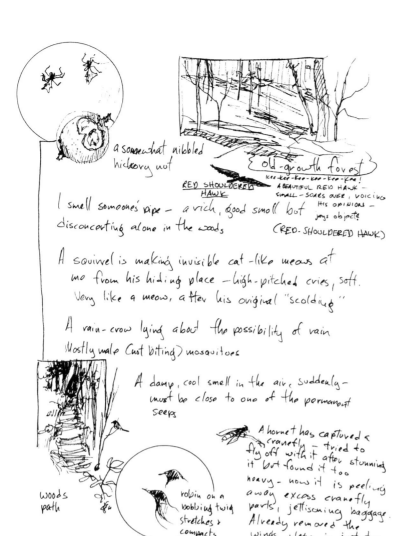

a somewhat nibbled hickory nut

Old-growth forest

kee-keo-keo-keo-keo-kae!

RED SHOULDERED HAWK

A BEAUTIFUL RED HAWK — SMALL — SOARS OVER, VOICING HIS OPINIONS — jays object!

I smell someone's pipe — a rich, good smell but disconcerting alone in the woods (RED-SHOULDERED HAWK)

A squirrel is making invisible cat-like meows at me from his hiding place — high-pitched cries, soft. Very like a meow, after his original "scolding"

A rain-crow lying about the possibility of rain

Mostly male (not biting) mosquitoes

A damp, cool smell in the air, suddenly — must be close to one of the permanent seeps

woods path

A hornet has captured a cranefly — tried to fly off with it after stunning it but found it too heavy — now it is peeling away excess cranefly parts, jettisoning baggage. Already removed the wings & legs in just two minutes — now he carries away his prize.

robin on a bobbing twig stretches & compacts his neck for balance

9-13. Naturalist/author/artist Ann Zwinger explores in her own special way, pencil in hand. These sketches were made with an HB pencil, which gives a good range of tones as well as control. *Tronador*, by Ann Zwinger. From *A Desert Country near the Sea*, 1983, Harper and Row. Reproduced courtesy of the artist.

9-12. Field sketchbook—as much written notes as drawn images.

9-14. Pale jewelweed grows just at the edge of the forest. A mechanical pencil with a B lead was used in this drawing.

9-15. A rotting log is the center of a mini-ecosystem in this field sketch. Keep on the alert for interesting subjects wherever you are. *Log*, by Gordon Morrison. Reproduced courtesy of the artist.

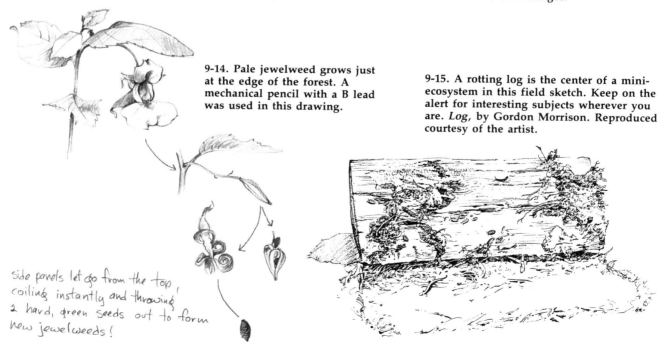

side panels let go from the top, coiling instantly and throwing 2 hard, green seeds out to form new jewelweeds!

9-16. This western box turtle appeared right in the middle of my street, providing a perfect sketching opportunity.

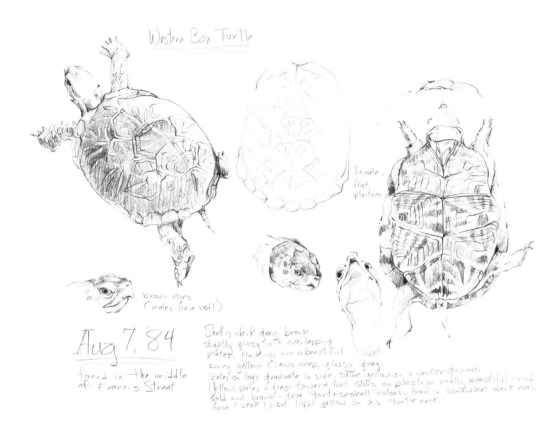

Western Box Turtle

female. flat plastron

brown eyes (males have red!)

Aug. 7, 84

found in the middle of Francis Street

Shell is dark gray-brown, slightly glossy with overlapping plates. Markings are a beautiful sunny yellow. Claws deep, glossy gray. Scales on legs graduate in size, same yellow on a darker ground. (Yellow patches always toward foot) Colors on plastron really beautiful-rich gold and brown - true "tortoiseshell" colors. Head is somewhat dark near nose (beak?) but light yellow on his "turtle neck."

Habitat is worthy of study no matter where you are. Not only your entire home territory but mini-ecosystems can be drawn and studied. In my immediate locale I can choose to study a river ecosystem, a swamp, an old-growth forest, a second-growth forest, or a pond, all with their own denizens, plant system and bird life (Fig. 9-13). Even a kind of miniclimate will be in effect, although the overall weather pattern for our part of the state may be fairly consistent. The forest is often cool and very dry. The river valley, on the same day, may be humid and warm. These differences affect the kinds of flowers and plants that grow, which in turn affects the kinds of animals that frequent the various habitats (Fig. 9-14). The woods are full of oak trees, woodpeckers, flickers,

squirrels, and, occasionally, deer and turkey (Fig. 9-15). In the spring the river valley attracts hordes of goldfinches that will feed on the abundant weed seeds. Robins flock to pull worms from the soft alluvial soil and eat the abundant wild grapes in the fall. The river itself is busy with fish, crawdads, frogs, water striders, damsel- and dragonflies. Life is more visible here than in the forest, and each place is endlessly fascinating. The pond shares some aspects of the river's system but not all, and the swamp is perhaps the most active of all, at least in microscopic life. What amazing abstracts can be drawn from these miniature creatures in their watery milieu (Fig. 9-16)!

Climatic changes, changes of season, and weather patterns that affect this area are wonderful to

sketch. There is a saying about midwestern weather: "If you don't like it, stick around. In five minutes it'll change." This makes for interesting and dramatic cloud formations (occasionally *too* dramatic—I once watched a tornado sweep into town from my hiding place in a cleft between two huge limestone rocks). You may be able to record an ice storm, a snowfall, a spring rain, a drought's crazy-quilt cracks in dried mud, a dust storm, a rainbow, a downpour. Tropical climates, arctic climates, temperate climates—all make interesting subjects. A field sketchbook is the perfect place to record these happenings initially, and they may end up in your paintings of fog or snow or a summer shower with a new authority and presence for having been experienced directly.

CHAPTER TEN

The Camera as a Tool

10-1

Unless you are taking up wild-life photography profes-sionally—in which case the cam-era becomes your stock-in-trade, your life—the camera is only one among many tools artists have at their disposal, neither more nor less important than a pen or brush. A camera can act like a sketchbook, assuming you al-ready have a thorough grounding in drawing. It can stop action, work in rain or snow, zoom in to catch the close-up workings of waterfowl or animals (Fig. 10-3). It can also distort, beguile, and outright lie, so caution is advisa-ble. Use it with discretion, as an auxiliary to your sketchbook or field notes.

Because color film and available developing vary so widely in their ability to capture color accurately, it is best not to rely on the camera as your only color reference. In-stead, consider your color photos as "sketches," memory aids to re-turn you to the special magic of an October day mellow with the glow of oak trees or the fiery color of butterfly weed. Seldom will a color print capture the depth and variety of color in a fox's pelt or the bottomless black of its pupils. Your memory, honed and sharp-ened, must supply that informa-tion. Color prints may be more misleading than slides, but con-venience compensates for their in-accuracies. Many wildlife artists use black-and-white photos only, so they will not be tempted to copy the color in a photo. And copying is the biggest danger

when using photography—you have already *created* an image, captured on film. Why copy what the camera can do, and possibly do better?

Combine photos and sections of photos to achieve the desired composition. You are not limited to what you see before you. It is best to use a number of research photos and to use them as you do drawings from your sketchbook, a source of inspiration, a jumping-off point, a reminder; a beginning, not an end (Fig. 10-4).

Shooting Your Own Research Photos

Because they will serve to jog your memory of an initial experience, it is better to use your own photos

10-2. Working from a photo need not be copying. Compare the original photograph to the drawing (Fig. 10-1, facing page) to see where areas were emphasized, edited, or eliminated altogether.

10-3. A camera would be a useful tool to stop action, as for this lithograph. *Great Horned Owl*, by Charles Stegner. Reproduced courtesy of the artist.

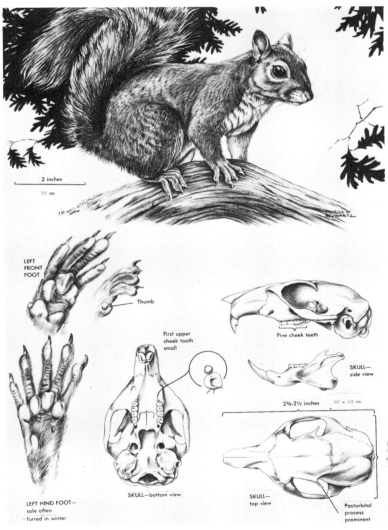

than someone else's; otherwise, you tend to create something twice removed from life.

Taking good photos is not so difficult to do. Cameras have improved as well as become simpler, so you no longer need to become a professional photographer with thousands of dollars' worth of equipment to obtain usable "sketch" prints. I recommend a single-lens reflex camera capable of accommodating interchangeable lenses, rather than one of the small instant cameras, since you will often want the versatility of the telephoto and wide-angle lenses, the ability to shoot close-ups, plus the creative convenience of being able to focus directly through the lens. With an SLR camera, what you see is what you

10-4. The artist used black-and-white research photos he shot himself to supplement field observation for these drawings. *Eastern Gray Squirrel*, by Charles W. Schwartz, in *The Wild Mammals of Missouri*, © 1959, 1981 by the curators of the University of Missouri. Reproduced by permission of the artist, the University of Missouri Press, the Missouri Historical Society, and the Conservation Commission of the State of Missouri.

10-5. Artists often use a photo ''morgue'' to help them accurately depict body characteristics or poses. *Ringtail Squirrel*, by Charles W. Schwartz, in *Wild Mammals of Missouri*, © 1959, 1981 by the curators of the University of Missouri. Reproduced by permission of the artist, the University of Missouri Press, the Missouri Historical Society, and the Conservation Commission of the State of Missouri.

will get, color variations excluded. A built-in exposure meter makes shooting usable pictures even easier. You will probably be able to get a quite serviceable outfit for between two hundred and three hundred dollars (extreme telephoto/zoom lens excluded). Charles W. Schwartz uses a Polaroid with black-and-white film for his photo sketches (Fig. 10-5). The choice is up to you. Practice a bit before you venture out on a special picture-taking safari, and you should come home with plenty of useful information. Slides do tend to be more color-accurate than prints are and have a finer grain for clearer enlargements, should you want them, but require a hand viewer at the very least to be of use as resource material.

Composing Your Photos

Consider several angles, both vertical and horizontal formats, plus a number of variables before you press that shutter. Of course, you will have checked to see that you have correctly set the ASA film-speed indicator to match the ASA speed of your film if you are relying on an automatic metering system, so the film will be properly exposed. It is often advisable to bracket several exposures of an important subject: that is, shoot one exposure just where your camera indicates it should be, one a full F-stop lighter, and one a full F-stop darker. That should produce a perfect—or imperfect but useful—photo (Fig. 10-7). (If not, have an expert check your camera and exposure meter.)

Unlike sketching, you cannot create a pleasing composition by moving that tree a bit off to one side or curving the river into the picture plane from the lower left—what is, *is*. But you can move yourself, change your vantage point, or change your format from horizontal to vertical or vice versa to give the most pleasing composition. Refer back to the sections on composition and format in chapter 2. The same rules apply as you shoot your research photos. Frame your composition in an interesting way, perhaps by including a foreground tree that seems to embrace the picture plane. Shoot your subject a bit off-center, and look for interesting angles. Shoot a few ''diagnostic'' as opposed to artistic shots simply to

obtain more solid information about your subject. And remember, nothing is set in stone in these photos. They are only sketches. If you use them as drawing references, you need not be restricted to a line-for-line reproduction—move things around to suit yourself (Fig. 10-6).

''Sketching'' Trips

One of the best times to use the camera as a tool is when you are on a tight schedule or a whirlwind trip, or when you are with others who tend to get impatient if you constantly stop to draw (an unpleasant situation all around and one to be avoided if possible). You may simply not have enough time to get down all the details you might need. Even a quick sketch is difficult on the freeway. Jim Hamil says he has been known to shoot out the car window while driving if he sees a particularly spectacular cloud formation and simply cannot stop. He may get a cockeyed angle or even the hood of the car, but he also gets his ''sketch.''

Unless you have made a field sketchbook a constant companion, you may not be able to get all the sketches you want as you travel. Drawing equipment is not always handy, but if you've made a habit of carrying your camera, you can always come back with some sort of visual record. In this case your camera *is* your sketching tool.

Rapidly moving objects also make the camera an invaluable sketching tool. We may travel to the west and see herds of pronghorn or American antelope, elk (wapiti), or buffalo that we could meet only in zoos or wildlife preserves at home (Fig 10-8). In their natural habitat, creatures are on their turf, as natural and unaffected as you are in your own home. If you have the opportunity to shoot a number of these

10-6. Even an imperfect exposure can be usable. This pencil drawing capitalized on the moody effect of the overexposed photo.

10-7. This pencil sketch was based only peripherally on the photo, rather than being an exact copy.

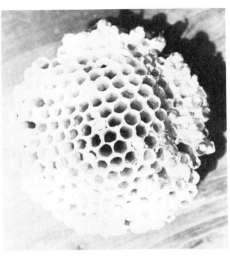

10-8. Photographic research is invaluable for rendering animals like this elk, done in oils. *November Elk*, by Bob Salo. Reproduced courtesy of the artist.

10-9. The photo here was quickly snapped in the Missouri Ozarks, and the scratchboard drawing was done later at home. The two-dimensional quality of the photo made it easier to simplify the natural rock bridge and the woodsy foliage behind it. Use photos to help you simplify what you see, especially necessary in scratchboard work. *Natural Bridge, Ha Ha Tonka*, by Cathy Johnson.

photo/sketches, you will have resource material for years to come. Remember, however, that an animal photographed in motion may appear distorted or blurred. Use a faster shutter speed to help stop action and avoid blurring. Available light may not be sufficient for the rapid shutter speed needed to stop action. You will need to use a number of shots to get to know the anatomy of your subject, research it in field guides, make a number of sketches, and *then* proceed (Fig. 10-9).

One final advantage: a camera attracts less attention (from humans) if you are shooting pictures in a park or other populated area than pulling out your sketchbook does. People are interested in artists, fascinated by real or imagined differences. If you prefer to be left alone, a camera is a useful tool. Still, it is only a tool, without the creative ability to choose and edit, move and accentuate that is yours with a sketchbook.

Using Other People's Photos

If you are planning to work from someone else's photo, be it old or new, remember that you are no longer recalling an experience of your own but responding to someone else's vision. It is, again, life twice removed. Some photos, of course, are so moving it is impossible *not* to respond, but you are responding to the beauty of the photographer's art as much as to the beauty of the subject itself. The work of great photographers has the power to elicit such responses.

Working from another's work puts you on dangerous ground. Not only are you at one remove from your subject, but you also may end up on the wrong side of the law. Copyright laws are stringent in this area. Unless you ask for and receive written permission from the photographer (and the

10-10. Because of a deadline, I was unable to shoot my own research photos or go where the ducks were. This photograph gave me just the information I needed. Notice how I chose to simplify and edit for my litho-crayon and Prismacolor pencil drawing. You might have chosen to use entirely different elements from this same resource. *Puddle Ducks*: photograph by Kevin Morgan; drawing by Cathy Johnson. Photograph reproduced courtesy of the artist.

publisher if the work appears in print), it is best to use another's work for information and inspiration only, not for direct copying. When I worked for a major greeting card company, we felt that everything was fair game for the artist's inspiration, and within ethical limits, it is. But do not risk a lawsuit, if you are working for publication, or embarrassment, if your work is exhibited and the source of your work is recognized.

When you are given an assign-

tonal values

linear

format or composition changes

10-11. Consider photo resources as much raw material as anything you find in the field. Experiment with value, format, composition, and technique. If you are working from a photo of an animal, move elements around as necessary to render a natural pose. Photograph by Kevin Morgan. Reproduced courtesy of the artist.

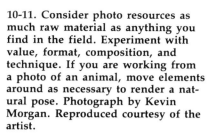

ment to render a specific subject and you are unable to take photographs yourself, a complete "morgue" of photos, drawings, sketches, and reproductions may be a lifesaver (Fig. 10-10). Most professional wildlife artists keep such a resource file and use it extensively. The details of a nose or hoof or horn may be impossible to obtain on short notice without your morgue. But I cannot stress too strongly the necessity of using these pieces as references only, not as a source to copy (Fig. 10-10). Change the animal's position, sketch and move things around until you have created something all your own, real and unique (Fig. 10-11). Some artists suggest reversing the animal's position in the picture if you must work from only one source, but mere "flopping" is not an adequate adaptation of someone else's work.

Although it might seem that a pencil or ink drawing would not be seen as an attempt to copy a photographer's work, such is not the case. Photographers put many hours and thousands of dollars into learning *their* art, purchasing their equipment, and traveling to remote locations, and the endless time and patience needed to produce fine wildlife photography cannot be overestimated. To have someone attempt an easy rip-off of their creative expression must seem thievery indeed. Imitation may be the sincerest form of flattery, but it does not pay a photographer's lab fees.

CHAPTER ELEVEN

Commercial Art

11-1

Drawing or painting from nature for your own enjoyment, for learning, as a contemplative exercise or simply as an excuse to get out into the world beyond your door is entirely different from commercial wildlife art or natural-history illustration. In the one case you are the final authority on what your finished piece will look like. If you wish to invent, distort, or introduce fanciful elements, go right ahead. In the case of commercial art, however, you are *not* the final arbiter: the organization that commissions the work is. Be it a wildlife magazine or other periodical, publisher of a textbook on biology or botany, or the conservation department of

your state government, perfection is no longer in the eye of the beholder but in the realm of the expert—and unless you have a doctorate degree in one of these specialized fields, you may no longer be the expert. Commercial art calls for meticulous attention to detail, including habitat, season, taxonomic characters, age of young or color phase of an animal's coat in relation to other seasonal elements. These things are not subject to interpretation; they are fact. Lighting is often prescribed in scientific or natural-history illustration; it comes from the upper left. While there *is* room for individual style, scientific accuracy is of paramount impor-

tance, and style must be subordinate to content (Figs. 11-2 and 11-3). This is no place for abstraction or impressionism.

Training for Commercial Art

Charles W. Schwartz is that special combination, an artist and a biologist (Fig. 11-4). Now retired, he was the chief artist at the Missouri Department of Conservation since the year before I was born, and much of my love for wildlife illustration as well as my interest in conservation came from the monthly issues of *The Missouri Conservationist*. When I contacted him some years ago for advice in getting the kinds of jobs he does

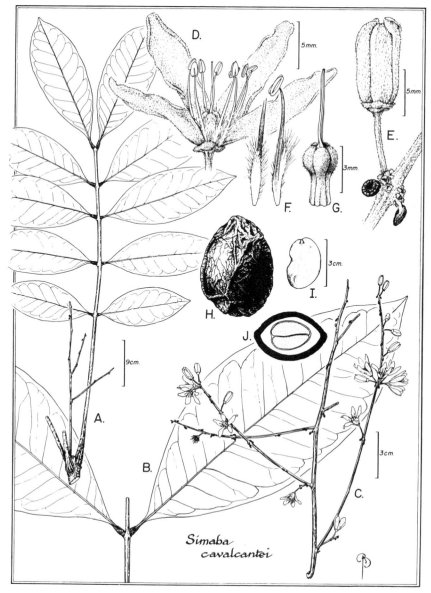

11-2. This careful pen-and-ink botanical has a beauty of its own, and is a good example of the kind of care needed for scientific illustration. *Simba cavalcantei*, by Bobbi Angell. Reproduced courtesy of the artist and the New York Botanical Garden.

are a great place to start. Unfortunately, in this country natural-history illustration is virtually ignored as a career possibility and—since commercial wildlife art is a difficult field to break into—few courses on field sketching or wildlife art are offered by major art schools or university art departments. Courses in field biology or botany may include a bit of information about keeping a field journal, but to marry the two areas of knowledge, you may have to become your own instructor. Fortunately, a number of good books are available on drawing and painting animals, plants, and landscapes, and some of these are listed in the Bibliography. The Guild of Natural Science Illustrators, P. O. Box 652, Ben Franklin Station, Washington, D.C. 20044, offers courses, seminars, and workshops in addition to a newsletter. Discussions of various techniques and contacts made through the newsletter may prove useful.

11-3. This shield bug and its prey were executed in opaque paints, which are often favored by natural-history illustrators. Notice the care taken with highlighting and markings. *Eyed Stink Bug and Potato Beetle*, by Gary Raham. Reproduced courtesy of the artist.

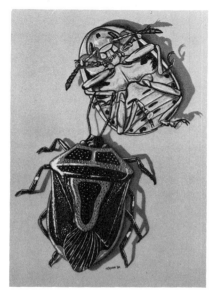

so well and obviously enjoys so much, his advice to me was to take some courses in biology, botany, field biology, or ecology, advice that I pass on here. If you do not have this kind of solid background yourself, find someone who does who is willing—and able—to critique your work not only from an artistic standpoint but from a scientific one as well. A college or university, a zoo, or your state's conservation department may be able to offer help (Fig. 11-5). When I was doing a watercolor illustration for *Sports Afield* on poison ivy, poison oak, and poison sumac, the Missouri Department of Conservation offered invaluable help in finding which varieties of poison oak grew where and how it differed from poison ivy (not much!).

Your local university or extension may offer courses you can take for credit or otherwise. These

11-4. These rough sketches show the genesis of the finished brush-and-ink-on-scratchboard drawing. Much careful planning goes into a drawing like this, from habitat studies to the animal's pose. *White-Tailed Deer*, by Charles W. Schwartz, in *Wildlife Drawings* by Charles W. Schwartz, © 1980 by the Conservation Commission of the State of Missouri. Reproduced courtesy of the Conservation Commission of the State of Missouri, the artist, the University of Missouri Press, and the Missouri State Historical Society.

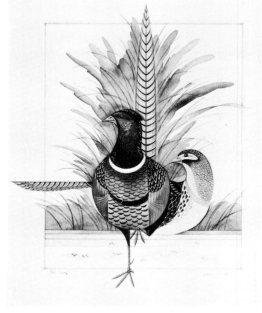

11-5. The folks at the Missouri Department of Conservation were very helpful in providing me with information for this piece. *Missouri's Endangered Predators*, by Cathy Johnson.

11-6. Research photos were used here as a basis for a more stylized presentation. *Pheasants —A Pair*, by John Stewart. Reproduced courtesy of the artist.

Finding Good Research Material

If you are working on assignment and accuracy is vital, the organization that commissioned you may have a variety of resources available for your use (Fig. 11-6). When in doubt, *ask*. You will save yourself a lot of work later if your art must be changed or done over. Museums, colleges, and universities may have stuffed specimens or study skins for close-up information. Consider, however, the relative skill of the taxidermist in the case of stuffed specimens. If a position looks stiff or awkward, do not trust it. Always check more than one source. Field guides vary in their body configurations, even for such common birds as robins. Check several sources, and trust your observations and common sense.

This is where your own photographs and field sketches will be of immeasurable help (Fig. 11-7). Your quick sketches may be no more than a few scribbled lines

made before the bird flew or the buffalo flopped in the tall grass, but they will be accurate, on-the-spot observations of stance, position, and configuration (Fig. 11-8).

Wildlife magazines, books, field guides—these are fine sources of research material, but again, do not be tempted to copy from any one source, or you may find yourself named in a lawsuit.

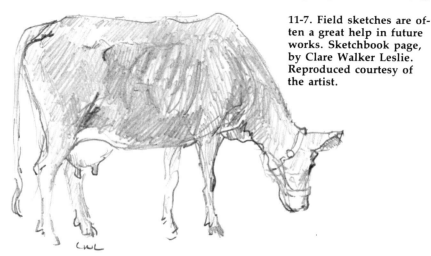

Style

Romanticizing or "prettying up" a specimen in a drawing can sometimes be a temptation. Here again, firsthand observation may prove to be your best friend. In many fields of natural-history or scientific illustration, sentiment may never be a problem. It is hard to imagine sentimentalizing a snake or bug or piece of coral (Fig.

11-7. Field sketches are often a great help in future works. Sketchbook page, by Clare Walker Leslie. Reproduced courtesy of the artist.

11-9). But those things that are traditionally perceived as beautiful (birds, butterflies, flowers, animals) or, worse, cute (baby birds and animals) come in for more than their share of distortion. If you are designing a greeting card, fine, make your subjects as cute and cuddly and misty as you like. But in most applications this treatment is not appropriate. See what is real, and do not be afraid to record it as it is (Fig. 11-10). For instance, in the Missouri trout stamp design, the trout is depicted in the fisherman's net. Many people prefer to think of wild creatures as free of man's intervention; in this case it was effective as well as appropriate to use the caught trout on a stamp sold to anglers.

A flower is really no less beautiful for having been nibbled by a hungry bug, and in fact it may be more truly poignant in reminding us of the frailty and vulnerability of beauty. A baby goose or fox kit really does have a softness about its down or fur, and in its eyes. The head *is* disproportionately large in relation to the body, the eyes are large and luminous, the feet are endearingly big—but it is not necessary or desirable to exaggerate these traits. The reality is touching enough and perhaps more so when we see it as it is. We do not need to pretend and therefore distance ourselves emotionally or psychologically.

The reality of the predator/prey relationship has a beauty of its own; carnivores are elegantly designed to their task. The red-tail hawk in Figure 11-11 illustrates that.

Such clear-eyed accuracy is important especially if you are working on a scientific illustration, which is to be used for *information* as well as decoration. If it is inaccurate—or the style you employ obtrudes—it is of no use to the scientist, and the result will be no more assignments for *you*.

11-8. The ink sketch shows one of the steps this artist takes in creating her natural-history paintings. She also shoots many research photos of habitat, background, and animals. While she is not a commercial artist per se, these steps are similar to those taken by someone in this field. *Sagebrush Shadows*, by Laney Hicks. Reproduced courtesy of the artist.

From Sketch to Finish

Once you have settled on your composition and accurately drawn your subject from your various resources, and you and your client are satisfied with your preliminary drawing or sketch, it is necessary to transfer it to the final working surface. In order to avoid damaging that final surface, by smudging it or abrading it from too much erasing and repositioning, you need a way to transfer with relatively little reworking. If

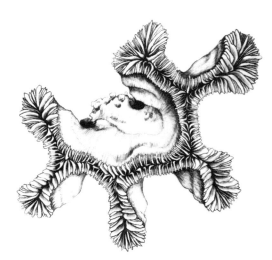

11-9. Although you would not sentimentalize a subject of this sort, you can use personal style to make it quite beautiful while maintaining the accuracy required in scientific illustration. This coral was carefully rendered with a technical pencil, with particular attention paid to lights and shadows. *Indo-Pacific Coral, Euphyllia Fimbriata*, by Pam Longobardi. Reproduced courtesy of the artist.

11-10. This painting was chosen by the Missouri Conservation Commission as its 1983 Trout Stamp. Trout stamp, by Terry Martin, © 1983. Reproduced by permission of the artist and the Missouri Department of Conservation.

your original drawing is small enough, an opaque projector may be a good choice, although I have found home-studio-sized devices to be frustrating at best. The original must be no larger than 6 inches square, or it will have to be transferred by one 6-inch section at a time. A dark or nearly dark room is a necessity, and focus may change somewhat as the projector's light source heats the device. Unless the artwork is placed under a sheet of glass, it may curl as it is being projected onto your paper or board, distorting the image. I had access to a professional "Lucy" (a lucidagraph, or indirect projector) when I worked for a large greeting-card company and later at a television station, so home models frustrate me beyond bothering with them.

If you share this frustration, you may resort to the grid system, a traditional and time-honored method (Fig. 11-12). Divide your sketch in half vertically and horizontally, then divide those halves in half. If necessary, continue to divide as shown until you

11-11. This painting of a red-tailed hawk shows the magnificent predator as it is. Notice the interesting negative shapes in this composition and how they focus the eye on the hawk. *Red-tail Hawk*, by James Faulkner. Reproduced courtesy of the artist.

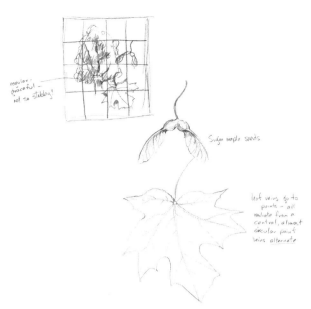

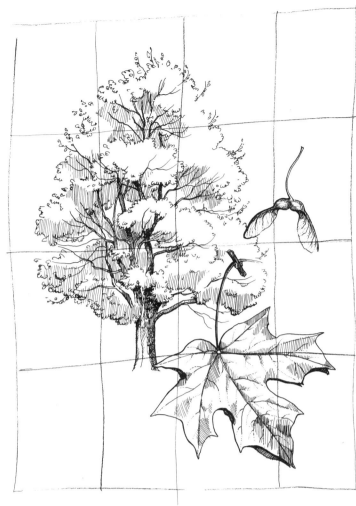

11-12. I work generally by eye, with a very loose grid system to help me transfer a small preliminary sketch to the finished surface without sacrificing proportion or composition. If I am doing a more demanding or complicated subject, I construct my grid with a ruler. These drawings show field sketches for the finished drawing, a composition sketch with a quick grid for transfer, and the completed drawing with a rough grid overlaid. Some elements were moved slightly for better effect. *Maple Tree and Keys*, by Cathy Johnson, © 1983 by the National Wildlife Federation, in *National Wildlife Magazine*, June/July 1983.

have a workable grid. This does not really need to be done with perfect squares, as long as your finished piece is in proportion to the sketch, as shown. Lightly divide your finished working surface in the same way. Now you can draw quite easily whatever shape is in the corresponding square or rectangle of the sketch, maintaining the same overall relationship between the parts.

I work best with a kind of direct, one-to-one system for most commercial assignments, however. Working usually from small thumbnail sketches, I enlarge them by eye onto tracing paper to the same size my finished work is to be. I might use the grid system, but in fact seldom do. I can redraw

or erase easily on heavy-duty tracing paper until the design suits me. If necessary I can even tape another piece of tracing paper over the original and redraw on it, changing what needs to be altered on this second sheet without worrying about erasing—and possibly tearing—the first. To see any errors in proportion or balance, it sometimes helps to flip the tracing paper over and check the design in reverse.

When everything is proportionally correct and pleasingly positioned, I tape the tracing paper drawing to my board or paper. You may wish to transfer by rubbing the back of the tracing paper with graphite where the lines are, then redrawing once your paper

is in place, but I prefer to use Saral paper for this purpose. This reusable, graphite-coated paper is slipped between the preliminary drawing and the final surface; then the design is retraced with a fairly hard pencil and steady pressure through all layers. Check under the edge occasionally to make sure your design is transferring properly. *Be sure* you have bought graphite Saral. I once borrowed a sheet of oil-based paper from a folk-artist friend and discovered the oil in her transfer paper resisted my watercolor washes. I had to start all over again, with a looming deadline. Also do not use typewriter carbon paper—it will interfere with your rendering media and is difficult to erase.

CHAPTER TWELVE

Other Techniques

12-1

Nature has been the source of inspiration for artists, designers, and craftspeople for millennia. The cave painters of Lascaux may have been among the first to depict nature; in the centuries that followed, the creative spirit surfaced in many ways and times and places (Fig. 12-2). The lace makers of France and Belgium incorporate birds, flowers, and animals in their intricate designs. Textile artists in India and the Far East have used natural subjects since the first calicoes and kimonos were printed, and tapestries of medieval times are renowned for their fanciful beasts and flowers. Italian glass workers make *millefiore* beads that look like thousands of tiny brilliant flowers; hence, their name. Cloisonné enamels are often adorned with floral or bird motifs.

Woodcarvers and sculptors also look to nature for inspiration. Henry Moore's works stand with a boldly monolithic presence, while Pablo Picasso's animal sculptures reduce his subjects to their very essence.

Look at the art of ancient Egypt, Africa, or South America. Fantastic beasts are intertwined with recognizable animals, and plants, trees, birds, and flowers adorn everything from pendants to pyramids. Many natural-history motifs in other cultures—as well as in our own—have symbolic or religious significance. The serpent may represent good or evil, healing or death, guile or knowledge, but almost always and in every culture, it also represents wisdom. The dove, of course, represents spirit as well as peace. The eagle is strength, freedom, wisdom—and our own national symbol.

Greek and Roman mythology abound in natural-history symbolism, as does the science of astronomy that grew from some of these myths. The Canis (dog) constellations; Ursa Minor and Major, the bears; Leo, the lion; Taurus, the bull; Corvus, the crow; Hydra, the sea serpent; Cancer, the crab; plus eagles, hare, fish, dolphins, and goats populate our myths and the heavens, and the earliest art that depicted them.

Throughout human history, natural forms have carried symbolic meaning. Flowers and herbs are prime examples: a lily may be used to represent purity; a rose, love. Early botanical drawings were often fanciful as well as decorative and informative: fantastic healing properties were ascribed to equally fantastic plants.

To come closer to home, consider the natural inspiration of

12-2. Knickknacks and decoys, such as this shorebird decoy, small Mexican pottery owl, and copper ''bug,'' are often based on natural forms.

12-3. The Inuit style inspired me to try this simplified and symbolized raccoon with ink on scratchboard.

some American quilt designs, such as ''Grandmother's Flower Garden'' and ''The Lone Star.'' Look at American Indian, Eskimo, or Inuit art, with their deep symbolic significance and simplified beauty, for examples of how nature is one with art and meaning (Fig. 12-3).

Nature and art are intertwined in every aspect of our lives, even in today's industrialized and commercialized society. Designs from nature are imprinted on bedsheets, curtains, clothing, and on kitchenware, mugs, and decorative knickknacks. Magazines are full of illustrations and ads that focus on nature (Fig. 12-4). Even our supermarket shelves are full of designs inspired by nature: look at the packaging of what we eat. And which of us has not spent some time in companionship with a teddy bear, that wild denizen of mountains and far places, now become a friend in brown plush (Fig. 12-5).

Thus, the forms of nature have enabled a very wide variety of artists and craftspeople to express their feelings about the world. Shown here and on the following

12-4. A .25 and a .35 technical pen were used for this illustration for my *Wild-Foods Cookbook*. This is not strictly *scientific* drawing, but a popular type of commercial natural history illustration. Reproduced courtesy of Stephen Greene Press, Inc.

← ragged blue flowers open in the morning, close by afternoon

edible root →

leaves deeply toothed

Chicory
dandelion-like leaves form a basal rosette

12-5. Using a soft lead pencil on drawing paper, I contrasted a teddy and a black bear in a whimsical vein. The current popularity of teddy bears prompted me to try this illustrative piece.

12-6. These shorn ewes were painted in the alla prima style in oil. The piece captures a sense of light as well as life. *Shorn Ewes*, by Charles Stegner. Reproduced courtesy of the artist.

pages are some examples of the range of media available to you. If you like, experiment with some of these to find your own way.

Oil Painting

Charles Stegner uses oils to render light as much as the specific subject of his paintings, and does so masterfully (Fig. 12-6). Robert W. Duffy's heavy impastos carry a sense of substance and volume within a strong composition (Fig. 12-7). Bob Salo paints oils of wildlife that stand out from the ordinary through imaginative use of color and value to express mood (see Fig. C-23).

Other opaque and semi-opaque media such as acrylics and pastels, are shown elsewhere in this book. Any or all of them should be explored to find the best way to express your own unique vision.

Prints

Printmaking is also a wonderful field for the artist interested in nature and wildlife, allowing a personal statement as well as the chance to use multiple images. My linoleum blocks of herbs have been used to imprint everything from notecards to clothing (Fig. 12-8). Ernest Lussier's lithographs are lively drawings done with a litho pencil (see Fig. 12-1). Other artists combine etching with natural forms impressed into the paper's damp surface to achieve interesting organic juxtapositions.

Pottery

Potters often use natural forms and decoration in their work (Fig. 12-9). If you like to work with your hands, the sensual medium of clay offers wonderful opportunities. Consider ways to shape or embellish your work with inspirations from nature.

12-7. Here, a heavy impasto technique expressed the rugged landscape with power and spontaneity. *Distant Farm*, by Robert W. Duffy. Reproduced courtesy of the artist.

12-8. Linoleum-block prints may be used to decorate everything from notepaper to clothing. I designed these herbal-inspired blocks for *Handmade* magazine. Reproduced courtesy of *Handmade*.

12-9. This nature-inspired tree-covered pot is shown with an odd antique claw-shaped candleholder. Pottery, by Dan Keegan. Reproduced courtesy of the artist.

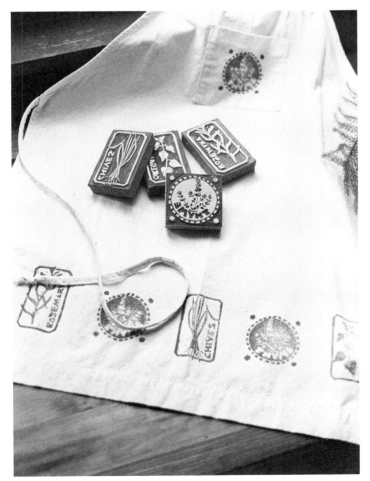

12-10. A Victorian beaded bag sprigged with roses.

12-11. A drawing of rosemary was designed to be impressed into the glass of Museum Editions, Ltd.'s bottle. This is one of twelve designs I did for this project. Reproduced courtesy of Museum Editions, Ltd.

Fiber Arts

Given the organic nature of their medium, fiber artists are often involved with natural forms and substances. Weavers who use wool, cotton, and flax may incorporate feathers, shells, stones, or driftwood into their work. In Victorian times beads were used with fabrics to embellish items from clothing to home furnishings (Fig. 12-10). Today we are more likely to see this inspiration expressed in beautifully knitted Fair Isle sweaters yoked with snowflakes or in a machine-quilted landscape shirt.

From Leaf to Glass

The glassblower's art is a fertile field. At the Renaissance Festival in Bonner Springs, Kansas, for example, an artisan in glass creates delicate birds, deer, and even dragons and unicorns as you watch. Recently I designed a series of herb bottles for Museum Editions, Ltd. These designs were imprinted into bottles made in origi-nal colonial molds, using authentic ingredients and colors. The rosemary bottle is shown in Figure 12-11.

The moral of this story—or this chapter, at any rate—is that you should not be boxed into any one way of creative thinking. Yes, this is a book on drawing and painting from nature, but it is intended to free you to see this beauty anywhere, all around you, to allow you to express yourself in whatever medium you choose, and for whatever purpose.

CHAPTER THIRTEEN

Art in Nature:
Finding a Different Level

13-1

Drawing and painting from nature can be much more than simply capturing a subject on paper or canvas. It gets inside you somehow, becomes a part of who you are—as an artist, as a person. I believe this can be a great benefit not only to you and to your art but also to those who see and appreciate your efforts—and in the end, to the planet itself.

Artists show the world as it is, in all its beauty and complexity—and its occasional ugliness—and perhaps, in doing so, help to preserve it. We inherit a delicate system, which includes built-in healing mechanisms, to be sure, but there is a point at which those systems break down.

By paying attention, we *focus* attention—whether on the finely balanced ecosystem of a tidal flat or a peat bog, on a fat black bear, or on the heart-stopping grace of a peregrine falcon. What we draw or paint, we take the time to see, really *see*, perhaps for the first time. What we draw, we learn to care about, and what we care about, we protect if we can. We become involved and may help others to do the same. Many wildlife artists have learned their images have power in the fight to preserve endangered species or public lands.

The images we make have the power to heal *us*, as well. Of course, there are the expected benefits of working in nature—fresh air, exercise, and so on. But, on a different level, our taking time enables our drawings and paintings to touch a place inside us. We slow down; time itself slows, or so it seems. Petty concerns fade. Even big problems seem to come into perspective when I lose myself in drawing a flower as it turns to the sun. Experience deepens. My work becomes contemplative, a kind of meditation more natural to me as an artist than breathing exercises or mantras.

Drawing as Contemplation
I am not the first person to suggest the connection between drawing and a meditative state, and I will not be the last. For many people

13-2. This study of long grasses has an almost hypnotic quality. *Grass Maze*, by Keith Hammer. Reproduced courtesy of the artist.

13-3. Many Oriental scrolls were designed as aids to meditation. The viewer was intended to enter into the scene, alone or with others. *Impressive View of the Go River*, by Ikeno Taiga. Reproduced by permission of the Nelson-Atkins Museum of Art, Kansas City, Missouri (Nelson Fund).

a kind of altered consciousness may be reached by contact with the brain's right hemisphere through drawing. A number of activities may also serve as a trigger for this cognitive, free-associating, fluid, and creative state. Music, poetry, and dance all serve to free a certain spirit, a different consciousness from our everyday, taking-care-of-business mode; for me, drawing does it best.

Although studies of brain hemisphere functions are relatively new, artists through the centuries have discovered that as they concentrate on their work, on the act of creating—and especially when they deeply identify with the object being drawn—they slip into a different way of looking at the world than the one they normally use. Breathing patterns alter, becoming for some deeper and slower. Others may almost forget to breathe as they work, fully identified with their subject and the process. If brain-wave patterns were tested during the act of drawing—and perhaps they have been—I would be willing to bet the patterns traced would be quite different from the norm.

Frederick Franck has written a number of books linking seeing and drawing to meditation. His works are essential reading for anyone interested in this subject, as are Betty Edwards's *Drawing on the Right Side of the Brain* and *Drawing on the Artist Within*. In Franck's books, drawing and meditation become one; in Edwards's, the right brain's creative mode is tapped to improve the ability to draw. Conversely, drawing can be used as a tool to reach a meditative state. In turn, the meditative can enrich your designs and paintings and inspire creativity (Fig. 13-2). Whichever mode you choose, whatever end you seek, the way in which you go about it is often a trigger to this altered state.

To begin with, be as still as possible. In the study of yoga, concentration on one's breathing is stressed; if that approach helps you, try to make your breathing slow and deep. If it simply distracts you (some people find themselves becoming so self-conscious about their breathing that they forget that it is, after all, on automatic pilot, and they become quite tense), try only to relax, perhaps closing your eyes (Fig. 13-3). *Tell* your body it is relaxed and calm. Imagine yourself in the act of drawing; imagine your drawing as it will appear on your paper.

Look at what you are drawing, your subject, with as few preconceptions as possible. See only how unique and beautiful it is, yet how perfectly ordinary; see beyond the ordinariness to its universality. Now begin to draw, tracing the contours or planes of your subject onto your paper. It does not matter whether it is a wonderful drawing or not. The act, the ob-

13-4. The beauty of shell fragments is captured here in colored pencil. When you are able to really see the world around you, fresh and unexpected subjects will present themselves to be drawn. Pencil drawing, by Mathilde Duffy. Reproduced courtesy of the artist.

ject, and your perception of it are what count now. You may find that you have never really seen, never really looked at your subject before, until you begin to pay attention, until you are fully open to what you see (Fig. 13-4).

There are many ways to reach this contemplative state; it is well worth some looking to find *your* way. The benefits are many—not only a state of altered consciousness, but a new way of seeing, of relating to what you see. Almost by osmosis, we learn from what we see most clearly. We take time; we form a relationship. It can be the beginning of a new way of working, a much more intense and personal way; it can be the beginning of a new life's work, a vocation rather than an avocation. You may find yourself becoming as much naturalist as artist; I did.

Finding a Special Place

You may find that you have a special affinity to a particular place—a certain area of the country where the light is clear and pure, a dramatic scene, a broad vista (Fig.

13-5). You return again and again, making sketches, taking notes, shooting research photos. John Stewart, whose landscape painting of New Mexico appears in Figure C-25 in the color section of this book, feels this affinity for the southwest. The way he has learned to see in terms of sharp contrasts of light and shadow because of this affinity affects all of his art, whatever its subject. Many wildlife artists love the west or Alaska for the superb opportunities to observe and paint animals (Fig. 13-6); others are drawn to the coastal areas or the boundary waters. The love you feel for your own special place will be evident in your work, eliciting a response.

Even if you never leave your home state, you can find opportunities to work from nature, and in fact an area that is easily accessible, that can be visited again and again on a regular basis will allow you to discover small serendipities, wonderful, unique secret pockets of beauty you did not imagine existed (Fig. 13-7). I have developed such a relationship with a small-town park not three blocks

13-5. A special time and place are captured here in watercolor. *Rising Trout*, by Thomas Aquinas Daly. Reproduced courtesy of the artist.

13-7. My backyard herb garden was the source for the subject of this ink drawing. *Fennel*, by Cathy Johnson. Reproduced courtesy of *Early American Life*.

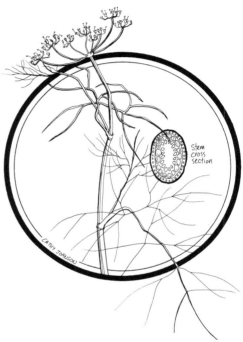

13-6. A fully antlered elk (wapiti) shows one reason many artists gravitate to the west. *Early Morning Light*, by Robert Salo. Reproduced courtesy of the artist.

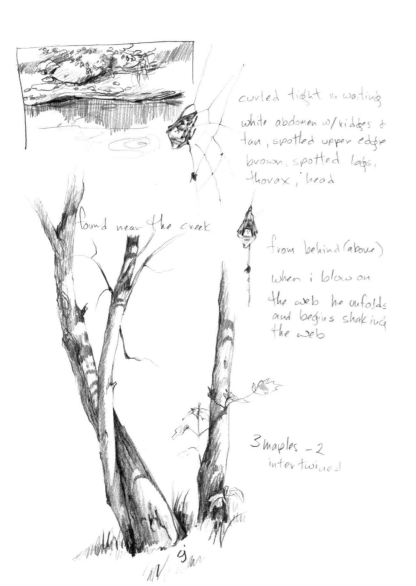

curled tight in waiting

white abdomen w/ ridges &
tan, spotted upper edge
brown, spotted legs,
thorax, head

found near the creek

from behind (above)

when i blow on
the web he unfolds
and begins shaking
the web

3 maples – 2
inter twined

Back Porch
Begonia
(an friend!)

13-8 and 13-9. Sketchbook pages.

from my home and have been pleased to explore a variety of ecosystems with my field journal and pencil: old-growth forest, creek banks, second-growth woods, swamps, dry clay cliffs and damp, mushroom-covered forest floors. It is a rare day that I do not discover something new along with the pleasantly renewed relationship with an old friend (Fig. 13-8). Sketching opportunities are limitless: turkey vultures, owls, and hawks share the area with songbirds of all kinds. Deer, raccoon, opossum, squirrel, and rabbit populate the park, and the creek banks are home to no less than four kinds of herons: great

blue, little blue, green, and black-crowned night herons. Wildflowers dot the park from late February to snowfall in November. Mushrooms and ferns of many varieties offer inspiration, and landscape opportunities are varied and interesting. At least once a week I try to walk as much of the area as I can, poking beneath leaves for mushrooms, investigating mammal signs, craning my neck to sketch a barred owl mobbed by songbirds. Almost every town I have visited has set aside a piece of land ripe for such study, and if not, the country is not so far away.

Paul Gauguin had his tropical

paradise, Claude Monet his lily ponds. George Caleb Bingham painted the American frontier; Grant Wood, rural America. Rembrandt loved the flat landscape of his native Holland. Andrew Wyeth paints New England, Georgia O'Keeffe portrayed the stark New Mexico landscapes. You can find your *own* special place, adopt it, and make it your own. Nature is not limited to the grandeur of the Tetons or the mystery of the Everglades. Nature is in your neighborhood park or natural area, a vacant lot, your own backyard, your potted plants and house pets (Figs. 13-9 and 13-10). Any area you love and see

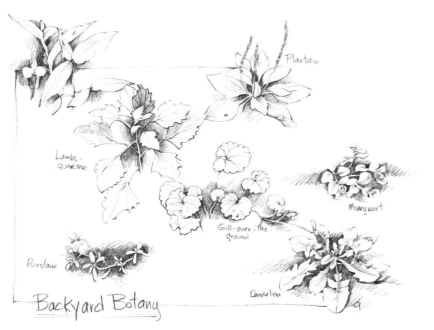

13-10. My own backyard is a microcosm of the larger, weedy world.

often can become this special place, a place you will learn from, a place where you will grow as an artist as you explore its beauties—however tiny—time and time again. Designers find inspiration in the patterns of the shadows on their own back fences. Familiarity does not necessarily breed contempt—it also engenders knowledge, contemplation, respect, relationship.

Forming a Learning Relationship With a Particular Place

When you go on sketching trips, whether day trips or vacations (unless you are fortunate enough to visit often and at all seasons),

you are limited to the time and season and weather, the habitat and creatures that occupied that small piece of Earth at the same time you did (Fig. 13-11). I will always envision Yosemite in the spring, full of light and the scent of flowers—an incredible sight and one worthy of many paintings. But although I have marveled at photos of Yosemite in other seasons, I could never paint the park in winter or at night with any degree of authenticity unless I had seen and felt and experienced these things for myself. I do not know what creatures populate an autumn night or a winter morning. I do not know what flowers bloom in August. *The Moon and Half Dome* belongs to Ansel Adams, not to me.

But a place with which we *are* able to form a learning relationship can teach us volumes. As we become intimate with its dawns and sunsets, noons and midnights, we begin to develop a feel for authenticity (Fig. 13-12). I *know* what walks the creek banks here. I have seen the herons and badgers, raccoons and deer. I can draw these things and know they look and act ''at home.''

We are infinitely enriched by this experience. Our knowledge grows as our consciousness expands. We are able to go far beyond a simple drawing of an animal or tree—*that* we could copy from a field guide or magazine. Experience, personal and deep, shows in a person's work (Figs. 13-13 and 13-14). Think again of Wyeth's Maine or Monet's lily ponds. They knew these places well.

Moreover, in becoming intimate with a particular slice of earth, we may find we know more of its life and ecosystem that we realize. We may come to understand more about how it works than any scientist. We may be able to contribute—in a small way—to a body of knowledge that could

13-11. The bottoms along the Missouri River are a particular ecosystem that has much in common with alluvial plains the world over.

13-12. The artist has formed a close relationship with a particular place, learning the habits of meadowlarks. This stylized acrylic painting shows that close observation allows for a lot of creative latitude. *Singing in the Rain*, by John Stewart. Reproduced courtesy of the artist.

Gall

Nov. 9, '82 –
Martha Lafite
Thompson Nature
Sanctuary –

leaf coiled like a
sea shell

warm, beautiful,
cloudy mostly

we lay on the
grass & watched
the mackerel sky,
while I drew the
curled leaf

13-13. I often go to a nearby nature sanctuary in Liberty, Missouri, to get away, sketch, and learn from nature.

13-14. The artist has translated something special in the play of light and shadow on two deck chairs. Learning to see in any environment is invaluable. *Uncle John's*, by Charles Stegner. Reproduced courtesy of the artist.

13-15. Drumlin Farm in Massachusetts affords naturalist/artist Clare Walker Leslie numerous subjects. Reproduced courtesy of the artist.

13-16. Drawing these nearby woods—the local wilderness —has become my vocation.

benefit our earth and our fellow man in many ways. Many artists have found that what started out as a simple wish to draw has grown into a lifelong concern to *preserve* those same subjects. Exploring and drawing this slice of earth may well become our vocation (Figs. 13-15 and 13-16).

Into the Woods

A learning place for me, one where I can reach a contemplative state, is the woods (Fig. 13-17). Of course, "woods" here is only a metaphor for nature. If you pre-

fer the seacoast, mountains, or desert, go where you are most in tune with yourself and your environment. The "woods" are handy to my home; if I lived elsewhere I would go into the desert or to the beach.

There are fewer distractions in nature—at least fewer man-made distractions of the sort we expect ourselves to cope with, *do* something about. There are no telephones, delivery men, deadlines, business meetings, laundry baskets, golf dates, or dirty dishes in the woods. We can become detached more easily from expecta-

tions of ourselves as well as demands on our time (Fig. 13-18). Those things will get done, or they will wait. But in addition, there is something more in the woods. David Rains Wallace, naturalist and writer, says that "wilderness generates mythological thinking; it leads the mind back to stories of origins and meanings, to imaging the world's creation." It is also a place where thoughts flow more freely, unobstructed; where words write themselves on paper without my having to search dryly for them; where images appear in my

sketchbook with a freshness, a life, a sense of light lacking at home in the studio (where such things must often be done for a purpose, a deadline—a paycheck).

Being quiet in nature is altogether different from being quiet in your own home. Here, you are not your everyday self: creature of habits, person of means, victim of circumstance, wife or husband, mother or father, doctor, lawyer, Indian chief. You can become one with what you see and hear and feel if you are simply quiet and let it flow into you (Fig. 13-19).

This peaceful aspect of nature is healing. Frazzled nerves, too many deadlines, and too much pressure can result in burnout. Going into the woods can be an antidote. Gordon Morrison believes his field sketches have a therapeutic effect (Fig. 13-20). These may not be intended for publication—they may have no intended purpose at all. They are simply done for their own sake; in my case I would have to say for my sake as well.

Nature teaches more about drawing and painting from nature than any book can. Train yourself to be still, to observe (Fig. 13-21). See how the sun shines through a morning mist; how a tree grows, springing from the soil; how light filters through a creek to dapple the pebbly bottom or shines through a scarlet leaf. Feel the rac-

13-18. Naturalist/artist Gordon Morrison speaks of using his field studies as meditative exercises. When he is tense or harried, he takes pencils, paints, and other equipment out into nature. This acrylic study is a case in point. *Great Blue Heron*, by Gordon Morrison. Reproduced courtesy of the artist.

13-19. I lost myself—and my various concerns—as I painted this unfinished study of fall fruits and berries.

13-20. Gordon Morrison is able to see things with a fresh eye in the field. He used a 2H pencil in this study of a barn swallow and slanting shadows. *Jackson, N.H.,* by Gordon Morrison. Reproduced courtesy of the artist.

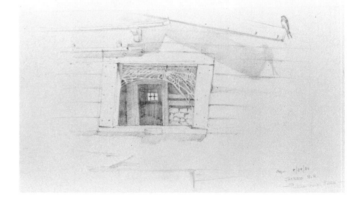

13-21. This artist has used a special kind of "seeing," based on many hours in the field, to capture this moment. His pointillist technique is also conducive to lengthy contemplation. Untitled, by Blaine Billman. Reproduced courtesy of the artist.

coon's hunger as it searches beneath the rocks at streamside for breakfast. Look at how a turtle's legs are perfectly constructed to contract neatly into the shell when necessary, yet carry him around with surprising swiftness and strength. Recognize how extraordinary the ordinary actually is (Fig. 13-22).

In a sense we are all pilgrims. Not the traditional black-clothed, white-collared figures from a Thanksgiving cartoon, but seekers, wanderers, hungering for manna we somehow know is to be found in the woods. As artists, this hunger is sharper than with many. It is an old hunger; we know it well. Each time we approach a blank piece of paper or

13-22. This watercolor takes a fresh look at a familiar subject. Washes were lovingly and slowly built up to produce this painting. *Asparagus*, by Peggy McKeehan. Reproduced courtesy of the artist.

13-23. This watercolor of trees by a river conveys peace. A meditative approach may help you to see, experience, and capture on paper nature's serenity. *Genessee River Bank with Light Snow*, by Thomas Aquinas Daly. Reproduced courtesy of the artist.

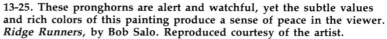

13-24. Lines and planes were explored carefully as I drew this fossilized turtle shell. I had never really noticed how the various plates and ridges fit together until I began to pay attention and draw.

13-25. These pronghorns are alert and watchful, yet the subtle values and rich colors of this painting produce a sense of peace in the viewer. *Ridge Runners*, by Bob Salo. Reproduced courtesy of the artist.

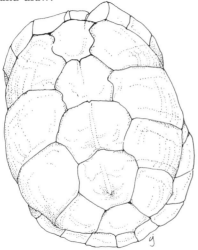

canvas, each time we take up a brush or pencil, we feel the pangs touch us. We search for expression, for beauty, for life. In the woods we are all wanderers, sojourners (Fig. 13-23). We travel to what may truly be a holy place, to find what may be there, what may become a part of us.

This attitude is a natural one for artists. We are always seeking the perfect pencil, the perfect brush, the perfect line (Fig. 13-24). We are always looking for ways to become catalysts, to take what we see and feel and experience and let it pass through us to our paper (Fig. 13-25). Like alchemists, we hope to take the raw material and turn it into something new, but in nature the reality is the gold and all too often *my* efforts, at least, are the dross. The humility we learn from our efforts is what turns us into true pilgrims. A lifetime of seeking is not too much, and the journey is always absorbing, fascinating, challenging. We enter the woods with our eyes and hands and art supplies, hoping to find treasure and knowing we will return changed, touched, calmed.

CHAPTER FOURTEEN

The Artist's Scrapbook

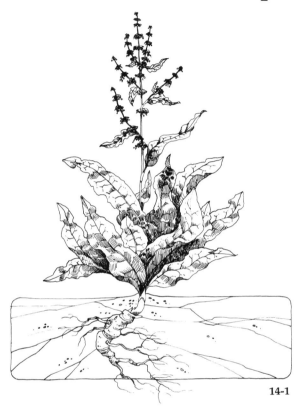

14-1

Artists are a wonderfully articulate lot, at least when talking about what concerns them most intimately: their work. Work touches all aspects of our lives, and whether we are inclined to careful, scientific renderings or splashy washes, delicate pencil drawings or heavy impastos, it is related to how we see ourselves and the world around us.

In this chapter are works and words of a few of the artists who draw and paint from nature. The differences as well as the similarities among them make fascinating reading.

Ann Zwinger
Ann is an artist, writer, and illustrator (Fig. 14-2).

I am an old-fashioned generalist naturalist who believes that being a naturalist solves all problems and cures all ills, is good for insomnia and hangnails, and offers the best of all possible worlds. I am also an old-fashioned illustrator, born with a pencil in my hand, drawing before I wrote. Now they are inseparable: what I draw becomes what I write and what I write is what I draw.

I am a generalist, fascinated by all things, whether they crawl, hop, skitter, or fly, or are rooted or rootless. I'm a basic wanderer because that's what naturalists do—they wander. Wandering is the pursuit of happiness from east to west, north to south, bending and stooping, examining and discarding, pausing, enjoying, not going anywhere in particular except down a beach or around a pond. There is an impeccable order in the way in which the dragonfly's wings clatter, the water strider creases the pond, in the way the lizard skitters and the kestrel stoops, in the way a stalk of grass scribes arcs in the desert sand.

For any one of those things there is a volume to be written. But if the drawing is right, it can be said in a few words, in the turn of the leaf and the shine of a pine needle. A drawing ought to say that there are *good* things going on in there, ticking away in leaf vein and heartwood.

You never know something until you draw it. And you've never written it until you've drawn it, even though the drawing may never reach paper. It's the thoughtfulness that counts.

Charles W. Schwartz

A mentor of mine, as mentioned earlier in this book, Charlie is an artist and a biologist. He knows what an animal is doing, why, and at what time of year, and can make it come alive. The beauty and life of his work makes it look easy (Fig. 14-3).

How do I work? I guess I can only say I try everything. I sketch from life when I can but often it isn't possible for the wildlife subject I need, that is, to make the sketches when I have an immediate need for something. The best source of reference for me is my own file of photographs. I rely on these almost entirely, although I do sometimes look through my morgue of clippings for ideas. I keep a field journal, but it covers a great many subjects in addition to art. I find it a ready reference for many reasons.

In my case I probably draw more than I paint—for one reason, because it is faster. A painting takes more time all the way around, and especially for oil paints to dry.

As to tools, I recommend that all wildlife artists draw first, then use paints or whatever other medium they may wish later. My most recent efforts have been sculpting

14-2. *Monarch*, pencil, by Ann Zwinger, in *A Desert Country Near the Sea*, by Ann Zwinger, published by Harper and Row (1983). Reproduced courtesy of the artist.

and casting in bronze. Here I use my photographs for reference, draw what I have in mind, then do my work in wax. I consider drawing very basic. I must add that I am a professional biologist and feel that my knowledge and understanding of animals—behavior and anatomy—are basic in helping me execute my drawings.

Blaine Billman

Pen-and-ink is Blaine Billman's medium. He works slowly and carefully in a pointillist technique (Fig. 14-4).

I work in pen-and-ink because the sharp contrasts and strong definition in line excite me. Pen-and-ink is perfect for these: you can take the softest imaginable texture, and if you break it down far enough, you'll find that it is defined by very distinct and precise lines, however minute they may be.

I love the challenge of ink, taking it to extremes that people find hard to believe. It makes me a magician in a sense, because I take a deep, rich black and cre-

ate the illusion of multiple shades of gray. I believe it makes me a better artist because there is little or no color to mask a bad drawing. Working in black-and-white helps me to "see" in a way that is not normally associated with wildlife art. The emphasis turns away from the appealing colors of nature to the fascinating variety of textures and patterns. You learn to see as a fox might see.

There are a few elements that I believe are absolutely crucial when it comes to making the actual drawing. First off, there is no *substitute* for field research. You can have all the books, and photographs, and mounts, etc., in the world, but they will not give you near the insight obtained by even the briefest encounter in the wild. Through that you come into a personal relationship with your subject. You are no longer merely an illustrator, but you become something of a window through which your viewers can share in the private, spiritual world of the wild.

In my own drawing the steps are relatively simple. In the first place, I never draw anything that I haven't seen in the wild. I pre-

14-3. *Raccoons*, brush-and-ink on scratchboard, by Charles W. Schwartz, in *Wildlife Drawings* by Charles W. Schwartz, © 1980 by the Conservation Commission of the State of Missouri. Reproduced courtesy of the artist and the Conservation Commission of the State of Missouri.

14-4. *Legacy of Sam Hawken*, pen-and-ink, by Blaine Billman. Reproduced courtesy of the artist.

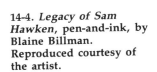

14-5. *Resting Squirrel*, pencil, by Sharon Stolzenberger. Reproduced courtesy of the artist.

fer to work from my own photographs and supplement these with mounts, molds, study skins, books, etc.

I have usually worked out the idea in advance and then go out and gather the research material for it. Occasionally it's the reverse. I begin with a very simple pencil drawing of the main subject and then establish in my mind where everything else in the picture will go. Then I will ink in the main subject and develop the scene around it, usually working from objects in the foreground on back. I work almost exclusively with a Hunt crow-quill and will sometimes use a razor, knife, or needle to scratch into the ink for effect.

I use a great deal of pointillism, which is very time consuming but versatile. One thing I never do is crosshatch because to me it disrupts the natural flow of line.

My drawings take tremendous amounts of time to complete. The quail drawing, for example (Fig. 13-21), took nearly 600 hours. There is a positive side to that, however. All the time I am drawing, I am thinking about the next piece and ways of putting it together. It is my idea time . . . my mental exercise program.

Sharon Stolzenberger
Professional artist Sharon Stolzenberger's approach is totally different from the previous example, yet just as effective (Fig. 14-5).

I work primarily in watercolor because I find it to be a very exciting, spontaneous medium in which to capture the vitality and alive-ness of my subjects—wildlife. I like to work loose, and I use a wet-on-wet watercolor technique in most of my paint-

ings because it allows me to focus on the essence of the animal, the freshness and "feel" of the animal, rather than trying to recreate something extremely photorealistic. I do my sketches from life in much the same way, preferring to start with loose, broad strokes, then adding refinement and minimal detail. I work from life as well as taking all my own photographic reference material. I work from both, but mainly from my photos when I am working in my studio to produce a finished painting.

I paint wildlife simply because it's fun and I enjoy it. There is such a wealth and overabundance of colors, textures, and shapes in nature that it's a constant stimulation of possibilities.

Although my formal education and background have been in commercial art, my interest in painting wildlife is parallel with my interest in environmental issues. I've been active in the Sierra Club and the Cincinnati Zoo; I support the Environmental Defense Fund, National Wildlife Federation, Greenpeace, and Nature Conservancy, to name a few. I regard my artwork also as being an educational tool through which people can come to appreciate nature and wildlife. I do art shows and outdoor art fairs as my main source of income now, and this allows me to come in contact with a lot of people.

Bobbi Angell
The overall spectrum of wildlife and nature drawing encompasses many individual fields of interest. Bobbi Angell is a professional illustrator whose pen-and-ink drawings of plants appear in many scientific journals (Fig. 14-6). Bobbi enjoys painting similar subjects in watercolor from her own perspective as well. Here she describes the work of a scientific or natural-history illustrator.

While working for a B. S. in botany, I became interested in the artistic opportunities within the field and decided to pursue a career as a botanical illustrator. I work as the staff illustrator for the New York Botanical Garden, a position I have held since 1978. My illustrations are used in the descriptions of new species and in regional floras.

In pursuit of taxonomic botany, collectors gather plants in the field, press and dry them, and return to their offices to study them. Little actual research is done in the field. My romantic notion of an artist sketching alongside a botanist in the tropics quickly faded, but not my interest. I try to spend spare time sketching and observing plants in the field for my own education and pleasure, but my scientific illustrations are always done from flat, brittle, and often ugly specimens. Under the best conditions the collector will provide Kodachromes and pickled flowers to help me. It is my job to enhance the botanist's written description with an illustration that describes an ideal species. Each drawing is a composite of several specimens; leaves from one, flowers from another. Taxonomic characters must be carefully depicted, which usually means the inclusion of microscopic details. Unless pickled material is available, I boil flowers and other small parts to soften them and then carefully dissect them under a microscope, my eyes traveling back and forth from paper to scope.

I arrange sketches roughly on tracing paper for layout and then transfer them onto bristol board (Strathmore two-ply, plate finish) on top of a light box using a 2H pencil that can be erased later. After the botanist has approved my sketch, I ink it in with a crow-quill nib (Hunt 102) and Pelikan ink, working from the upper left

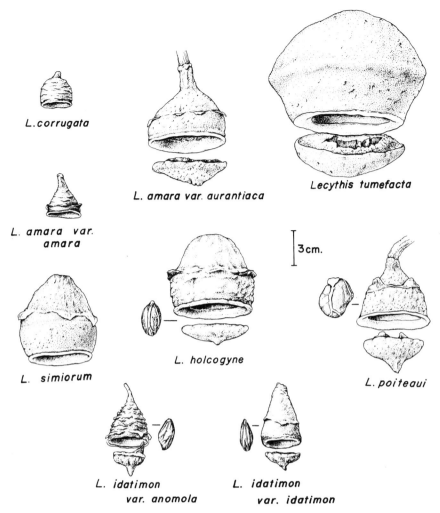

14-6. *Lecythis Seed and Seed Cases*, crow-quill pen and ink, by Bobbi Angell, in "Lecythidaceae of a Lowland Neotropical Forest" by Scott Mori. Reproduced courtesy of the artist, the New York Botanical Garden, and Scott Mori.

corner down. The plant specimen is always nearby for constant rechecking. Mistakes are corrected with an electric eraser and re-inked.

In contrast to my scientific illustrations in pen-and-ink, my watercolors are all done from live plants in my studio. Plants change and die as I paint, so the final picture ends up as a composite of different branches and flowers modified by memory and imagination. I paint the most ephemeral parts first (buds and blossoms) and then move on to the leaves and stem. I build up many thin dry layers of paint,

adding color until the right density and detail are achieved. My palette contains about fifteen colors of Winsor and Newton tube paints; my paper is Arches 140-pound hot press.

Carol Sorensen

Wildlife artist Carol Sorensen works in a medium that is experiencing a well-deserved surge of interest: colored pencil. Her drawings capture a sense of life in a unique way (Fig. 14-7).

In the past, wildlife art and realistic art in general were criticized for

14-7. *Fawn*, colored pencil, by Carol Sorensen. Reproduced courtesy of the artist.

being "illustrative." Luckily, all that is changing. My work is an unending search for knowledge about the natural world, not only how its creatures look but how they contribute to the overall scheme. For most of the last decade I have been exploring the North American continent and those animals most familiar to me. Still there is much to be learned within those perimeters. Few people in our society see wild animals up close, unless it is through the camera viewfinder or rifle scope. Beyond what a camera records, I am able to add my impressions of how the textures would feel if touched, and how the expression and gesture of the animal's eyes, face, and body reveal the place he occupies in his surroundings. While I feel for the endangered species, I respond most to those that are adaptable enough to move in alongside man when necessary, thus enriching our daily lives and

reminding mankind ours is not the only claim on the earth's resources.

While preparing to start one of my wildlife drawings, I may spend several weeks doing research, making preliminary sketches, jelling my ideas, and setting aside the drawing for a few hours or a few days to gain some distance and a fresh perspective. Preliminary sketches are worked in graphite pencil on tracing paper, which has a nice toothy texture. The sketch can be turned over to study the image in reverse. Adjustments can be sketched on the back and tried for effect without disturbing the original drawing, or a fresh sheet can be laid over the drawing and variations tried out without losing the original idea.

The sketch is transferred to a 100 percent rag mat board. Most of my work is done on rich, dark, natural-colored rag boards with untextured surfaces, since I enjoy

the effect achieved when light and color are built up on the dark surface. This negative ground visually recedes, and the drawing takes on a three-dimensional feeling, which adds to the lifelike effect of the animal I am trying to capture.

I use all the colors in my pencil set except copper, silver, and gold. Even orange, purple, and magenta are incorporated in small amounts into the drawings. The strokes of varying colors make a drawing exciting.

While colored pencils have been around for many decades, they seem lately to be rapidly growing in popularity as a fine-art medium. They are a perfect art tool. They come in a variety of beautiful colors, they are permanent, inexpensive, store easily without deterioration, require no elaborate tools, are easily erased, and don't smell, splash, or smear. They can be picked up for a few minutes' or a few hours' use without creative time lost in setting up or cleaning up afterward. They travel compactly and can be used anywhere. The artist is released from frustrations with lost time or muddied colors and is able to relax and produce free and expressive art.

I am pleased when I have captured a lifelike representation of one of the most interesting and beautiful things on this earth. After discovering each creature for myself, I ask no more than to have another human being respond with the same feeling of discovery.

Donna Aldridge

Professional artist Donna Aldridge feels much this same kind of excitement and immediacy when she uses pastels to capture her dynamic and exciting landscapes (Fig. 14-8).

Pastels are lusty and potent, rich in color yet sensitive to the subtlest

14-8. *Bottom Forty*, pastel, by Donna Aldridge. Reproduced courtesy of the artist.

nuances and most delicate shadows. They can generate the strength of a granite boulder and the wispiness of a passing cloud. Color can be sprinkled or exploded across the picture, embedding a fantastic mosaic of hues, layer upon layer, building a powerful image. Pastels seem the most immediate of all media to me. We need only grasp a stick of pigment in our hand and begin drawing, dashing, dotting, scrawling, rubbing, scrubbing, smearing, stroking, hatching color across the surface in joyous wild abandon or with precise and cautious intent.

I usually work my pastel paintings on sheets of beige 100 percent rag paper with an imperceptible tooth. I begin by marking off a 2-inch border area for testing or cleaning pastels, then lay out the composition and scrub in local color with soft pastels. I rub this into the paper and fix it,

establishing base colors and a fine tooth. Weaving strokes of closely related hues or values, often of low intensities, tingling fields of color begin to flourish.

When I see a scene to paint or etch that excites me, I "experience" it physically as well as visually—feeling the weights and movements of its dynamics, the interaction of the colors, the drama of its value patterns, the pulse of the textures and energy of the composition. I paint the picture in my mind again and again. Invariably, the better "understood" it is in my head, the more easily the picture flows onto paper or canvas or plate.

I believe it's important that we understand what elements we personally are responding to when we look at something that stirs our interest to paint. A snow-covered farm field by a wooded area may be seen in many different ways. One artist may stand

there seeing the strong contrast between brilliant lights and shadowy darks of the snow and trees, with the textures of the field stubble and the tree branches providing a subtle, brocade richness to the opposing tonal areas, creating a dramatic impact of values cutting across the picture plane. Another might be more aware of the space and distance as the furrows wind off quietly across the broad field, the trees dark and rich in the foreground and softened more and more by the haze as they circle behind the field, finally dissipating in misty layers of the background. Everything would be pulled together and softened by the hazy-bright overcast of the winter day. The focus would be on atmosphere, on mood. Still another person might be struck by the bountiful complementary color scheme of umbers, taupes, rusts, and ochres against cobalts, teals, mauves,

14-9. *Chill Factor*, oil, by Laney Hicks. Reproduced courtesy of the artist.

what I have seen—to share some vision of the world even though we are separated by time and space.

Laney Hicks

Laney Hicks works in oil and watercolor (Fig. 14-9).

I am primarily an animal artist, though I do people now and then. My family background is weighted toward appreciating animals—they were always part of our household and treated as equals, and we respected their right to develop their own identities. As with people, every individual animal in each species is different in personality and structure. It makes for a source of constant interest to me to observe the behavior of wildlife and domestic animals and then to portray that individual in its surroundings.

The second largest influence in my painting is Oriental art and philosophy. My design style is simple, with only a few elements (three to five) in each composition. The basic pattern is positive and negative space with the main subject, usually an animal, balanced with large, uncomplicated surrounding areas.

To be an animal artist, and do it with confidence and detail, I believe the artist should also be a photographer. Though using photos means there are certain inherent problems with distortion and flat images, they are invaluable references for subjects that do not stop and pose for long periods of time. I have a great deal of good camera equipment, and I emphasize *good*, because the quality of the photo will influence the painting. I spend 20 to 25 percent of my time in the field photographing animals and habitat.

In the planning process, my paintings are a composite of two

and grays in the woods and fields. Space and value contrast would play only supporting character roles to a vibrant patchwork of intensified colors playing across the landscape.

Sometimes I know almost immediately what is at play in a scene I want to paint. Other times I must look carefully, patiently, to

"understand" what I am responding to.

I don't know why other people paint and draw. For me there is, at least in part, a need and a desire to communicate with other human beings things that I have "seen/felt". I want, if only for a moment, for another human being to see his or her version of

14-10. *Elephant Shrew*, pencil, by Carolyn Dorsey Rathbun. Reproduced courtesy of the artist.

factors: good animal photos and my preference for Oriental composition. I do a series of small sketches in pen-and-ink, possibly fifteen to twenty, before deciding which one is most pleasing to me.

The next step is to draw the subject up to size and transfer it to the prepared Masonite board or watercolor paper. Sometimes I do a small watercolor painting in between the ink sketch and the up-to-size drawing to make sure my color composition will be attractive.

Carolyn Dorsey Rathbun

Carolyn Dorsey Rathbun is a wildlife artist (Fig. 14-10).

Traditionally illustrators have been looked down upon because they are said to be acting only as vehicles for the visual expression of someone else's ideas. While I feel this critcism ignores the technical abilities and intrinsic sensitivity so necessary in the visual expression of an idea, I do feel that there is a tendency, especially in scientific work, for illustrations to become lifeless and dull. Even though I have been trained to think and see as a scientist, I would like people to relate emotionally as well as intellectually to my work. To me, that is what art is all about. While continuing to do illustrations, I am trying to work in a less restrictive format and to incorporate new and different images in my drawings and paintings.

Mathilde Duffy

Artist, teacher, and scuba diver, Mathilde specializes in the myriad shells she finds on Siesta Key, an island off Sarasota, Florida (Fig. 14-11).

Drawing shells is a natural culmination of a lifelong attachment to the sea; an eye for fine detail, in-

14-11. *Fifteen Friends*, colored pencil, by Mathilde Duffy. Reproduced courtesy of the artist.

tricate design, and color patterns; and a longing to share unusual shells with others. After all, the rich textures and patterns of shells are among nature's most striking abstract works of art.

I block in surface areas with pastel pencils and work in the details with the various colored pencils. Each pencil handles differently. Some smudge better than others, some have more saturated color, etc.

The finest details are added last, and kneaded erasers pull out the last highlights.

John Stewart

John Stewart paints flat-plane landscapes of the southwest that glow like brilliant mosaic. He uses acrylics in an opaque manner to build flat areas of color that combine to create a harmonious whole. He also specializes in wonderful stylized bird paintings (Fig. 14-12).

I work mostly from photographs I have taken myself or ones I can use a portion of. I break this into shapes or patterns for simplification. This enables me to see

things in terms of flat shapes, then use that to build on. In a very real way, what I do is to work with lines and fill in the shapes, using light and dark, warm and cool to express a particular subject. It becomes my interpretation of things I see—the more I paint like this the more I *see* things in terms of shape. If something I see has an impact on me emotionally, I can take a photo of it and even if the shot doesn't come out with all the light and shadow and color, I am able to recall and recover the excitement. I can build it back into my painting. As long as I've had that experience, it is always with me—it just needs to be recalled.

I use flat shapes to express form, rather than a blended shadow shape—the juxtaposition of one form against another through use of color and light. To help me see shapes in these simplified terms, I often squint my eyes. Sometimes even when I'm in the middle of a painting I will squint at it to see if the light and dark patterns are working.

Clare Walker Leslie

Clare Walker Leslie is well known

14-12. *In the Swim*, acrylic, by John Stewart. Reproduced courtesy of the artist.

14-13. Field sketch, goat, pencil, by Clare Walker Leslie. Reproduced courtesy of the artist.

for her nature drawings and field sketches (Fig. 14-13). She has written and illustrated a number of books, among them *Nature Drawing: A Tool for Learning* (Prentice-Hall, Inc., 1980), *The Art of Field Sketching* (Prentice-Hall, Inc., 1984), and *A Naturalist's Sketchbook: Pages from the Seasons of the Year,* (Dodd, Mead and Company, Inc., 1987). Clare lectures and teaches as well as shows her drawings and paintings in various galleries.

I use drawing as a way of studying nature. It also provides me with a tool that is faster than writing when recording something of particular interest that I have noticed outdoors. As an artist, I find it exciting to see even the less showy events of nature, such as a beetle crossing the road or a squirrel maneuvering through the trees, and to be able to recount, in image and on paper, what I have seen.

The advantage of sketching over drawing is that you can record very rapidly what you are observing without concern for artistic detail. Getting the basic facts down is what counts. Therefore, because I do a lot of nature observing outdoors where things rarely stay still (and I do not wish to stay still either), rapid sketching becomes a more practical method than slower drawing. Often I barely look at the page while I rapidly set down what I see. Refinements on my sketches can be worked on if I desire when back in the studio.

I do believe that a firm grounding in the techniques of drawing is eventually necessary and that it takes years of practice to draw really well. With this in mind, I guess it is why I teach sketching to students more and more—because sketching does allow you to get something down on paper without getting hung up on creating a masterpiece. In sketching, there is usually more emphasis on *what* is being seen than on *how* it is being recorded.

If one is to draw nature with any degree of seriousness, it does become important not only to observe it for lengths of time outdoors, but to also go to zoos, nature/science museums, aquariums, and draw things that are less likely to run away. It is also necessary to draw from study skins, skeletons, taxidermy mounts, as well as from photographs. I tell my students to draw from whatever they can get their hands on provided it accurately represents the living creature in its natural state. (Sadly, many taxidermy mounts today in museums are old and in poor condition.)

I also value copying—to learn from the works of well-known wildlife artists—provided students clearly mark down that a painting or drawing was copied and who did the original. Since it is difficult to find good courses in wildlife drawing (nature drawing, natural-history drawing), I recommend students make studies of the art of such good "teachers" as Beatrix Potter, Ernest Thompson Seton, Toulouse-Lautrec, Francis Lee Jaques, Andrew Wyeth, or Robert Bateman. I learned how to draw animals and plants working long hours in practice and in getting help poring over and copying as many good artists' works as I could find. Eventually you will find your own style. But remember, it used to be the tradition to copy the master's style before you learned your own. Just do not call it your own!

To find good examples of nature drawing can be a challenge but well worth the hunt. Since art museums have yet to exhibit much wildlife art, your best bet is in book illustration and even sometimes in greeting cards. Libraries, bookstores, and used bookstores are my "art museums." Go to the nature/science and children's sections and look carefully at the illustrations. There is some very exciting nature drawing happening today, but you will have to do some research to find it. But do not despair; once you are on the path, you will see how fulfilling and fascinating an area of drawing it can be.

Whether I am using pencil, pen, colored pencil, or watercolors, I use my art as a way of connecting with the natural world, as a way of being with it for a while undisturbed, and as a way of creatively expressing for myself and for others what I have experienced. I suppose I perceive my art as being a mixture of the creative and the educational.

I would also like to mention that I am a wife and a mother, with a studio within my home (with work space sometimes relegated to the kitchen table, to the front yard, or to the car). Drawing nature as I do is a wonderful profession because I *can* do it anywhere and at any time. My sketch journals are full of notations (sometimes used in later drawings or paintings or illustrations for books) of birds seen out the bedroom window, objects collected from a walk, the family rabbit or ant farm, an insect on the bathroom window, or scenes sketched while traveling in the car. If you make a commitment to be always drawing and studying nature, then you can find subjects anywhere and at any time—and your powers of observation become much more acute and interesting.

Bibliography

These are a few of the books that you may find useful in learning to draw and paint from nature, whether you are interested in wildlife, botanicals, landscape, or an overall naturalist's view. There are a number of other excellent sources, and you may find I have excluded your personal favorite, but the ones I have chosen to include have been especially meaningful or useful to me.

Adams, Norman, and Joe Singer. *Drawing Animals*. New York: Watson-Guptill Company, 1979.

This book contains beautiful pencil drawings—the preliminary sketches are as interesting as the finished drawings.

Arnosky, Jim. *Drawing from Nature*. New York: Lothrop, Lee and Shepard Books, 1982. ———*Drawing Life in Motion*.New York: Lothrop, Lee and Shepard Books, 1984.———*Sketching Outdoors in Spring*. New York: Lothrop, Lee and Shepard Books, 1987.

These charming little books are full of Jim Arnosky's unique and sprightly pencil drawings. His keen observation of nature is worth the price of admission. He has written and illustrated a number of others; these just happen to be the ones in my personal library.

Blockley, John. *Watercolor Interpretations*. Cincinnati: North Light Books, 1987.

Blockley is one of my favorite watercolorists; his surety of handling is an inspiration. He never copies nature but, as he says, interprets it most beautifully. Any designer or illustrator should find plenty of ideas here; the landscape painter will find revelation.

Brandt, Rex. *The Winning Ways of Watercolor*. New York: Van Nostrand Reinhold Company Inc., 1973.

This is one of the classic watercolor books, full of ideas and techniques.

Couch, Tony. *Watercolor: You Can Do It!* Cincinnati: North Light Books, 1987.

For those who thought watercolor was too difficult to attempt, Couch's book is a revelation.

Daly, Thomas Aquinas. *Painting Nature's Quiet Places*. New York: Watson-Guptill Company, 1985.

Daly is a modern master of watercolor—his small landscapes and still-life compositions are an education not only in technique but in the less tangible qualities such as inspiration, with a kind of spirituality as well. I never fail to feel calmed when I look through this book.

De Grandis, Luigina. *Theory and Use of Color*. New York: Harry N. Abrams, Inc., 1986.

A thorough overview of color theory.

Dodson, Bert. *Keys to Drawing*. Cincinnati: North Light Books, 1985.

Though not largely concerned with nature, Dodson's book is an excellent guide to sketching techniques.

Edwards, Betty. *Drawing on the Right Side of the Brain*. Los Angeles: J. P. Tarcher, Inc., 1979.

Studies in right-brain creativity release the artist in all of us. Edwards's book is a revelation and a practical guide to tapping those inner resources in us all. It will be a modern classic.

Franck, Frederick. *The Awakened Eye.* New York: Random House, Vintage Books, 1979.

Any and all of Franck's books are worth the price of admission; this is my personal favorite. His work captures the spiritual rather than the technical side of drawing.

Gayton, Richard. *Artist Outdoors.* New York: Prentice Hall Press, 1987.

Gayton's book is a wonderful study of working outdoors in nature in the American West. The landscapes are especially useful to the aspiring artist.

Gurney, James, and Thomas Kinkade. *The Artist's Guide to Sketching.* New York: Watson-Guptill Company, 1982.

Gurney and Kinkade offer suggestions on sketching just about everything, everywhere, under all conditions. It's not only an excellent learning tool, but it's fun just to look at.

Hammond, Nicholas. *Twentieth Century Wildlife Artists.* Woodstock, New York: The Overlook Press, 1986.

Not strictly a how-to, this wonderful book examines the works of some of the best-known nature artists of this century. It overlooks most of the female artists, however, a sad omission.

Jamison, Philip. *Capturing Nature in Watercolor.* New York: Watson-Guptill Company, 1980.

Jamison's watercolor landscapes are inspirations.

Johnson, Cathy. *Painting Nature's Details in Watercolor.* Cincinnati: North Light Books, 1987. ———*Watercolor Tricks and Techniques.* Cincinnati: North Light Books, 1988.

My two watercolor books are quite different from one another—and from this book. They offer a number of suggestions not only for the varieties of techniques possible in the demanding medium of watercolor, but for sketching, composition, format, and the keeping of a field journal.

Johnson, Peter, ed. *Drawing for Pleasure.* Cincinnati: North Light Books, 1984.

The title of this book is quite apt; a pleasure it is, and so is this volume.

Jones, Franklin. *Painting Nature.* Cincinnati: North Light Books, 1978.

Jones's book covers a variety of media in handling the subject of landscape.

Leland, Nita. *Exploring Color.* Cincinnati: North Light Books, 1985.

Leland's book is an in-depth study of using and controlling color in your paintings.

Leslie, Clare Walker. *The Art of Field Sketching.* Englewood Cliffs, New Jersey: Prentice-Hall, Inc., 1984.

A wonderful introduction to the naturalist/artist's world, this book is a must for anyone truly interested in working from nature. Field sketching is a study in itself; Leslie does it justice here:
———*.Nature Drawing: A Tool for Learning.* Englewood Cliffs, New Jersey: Prentice-Hall, Inc., 1980.

This landmark book serves as an introduction to nature study through the discipline of art. Leslie's sketches and drawings are complemented by the text. She has also included the works of a number of other artists, from students to old masters, making this a most useful book. A must-read.

Malins, Frederick. *Drawings of the Old Masters.* Tucson, Arizona: HP Books, 1981.

This is not so much a how-to as an introduction to the drawing solutions of the masters.

Monahan, Patricia. *Landscape Painting.* London: QED Books, 1985. Reprint. Cincinnati: North Light Books, n.d.

The varieties of techniques for landscape painting described in this book are a wonderful source of inspiration for the designer and illustrator as well as the artist/naturalist.

Muybridge, Eadweard. *Animals in Motion.* Edited by Lewis S. Brown. New York: Dover Publications, Inc., 1957.

This is not a drawing book at all, but a sourcebook of thousands of photos of animals in motion. It is most useful when trying to find just the right pose for an active beast.

Nicolaides, Kimon. *The Natural Way to Draw.* Boston: Houghton Mifflin Company, 1941.

This is a classic; most of us cut our artistic teeth on its dog-eared pages.

One of the best all-around books on drawing to be found.

Pike, John. *John Pike Paints Watercolors.* New York: Watson-Guptill Company, 1978.

John Pike was a master of watercolor techniques; the man could paint *anything.* Whatever you might see in nature, from fire to storm to mist to an eagle soaring high or a deer in the woods, Pike could paint it in such a way that it looked easy—and *fun.* He expressed himself here in terms that communicate to the aspiring painter.

Reid, Charles. *Flower Painting in Watercolor.* New York: Watson-Guptill Company, 1979.

Charles Reid is one of our premier young watercolorists; his many books are not only extremely helpful but beautiful to look at. I recommend them all, but particularly this one for an excellent example of unsentimental flower painting.

Sims, Graeme. *Painting and Drawing Animals.* New York: Watson-Guptill Company, 1983.

These are beautiful watercolors with a real sense of life. Many of the finished paintings are really more like drawings done with paint, an interesting technique.

Sweney, Frederic. *The Art of Painting Animals.* Englewood Cliffs, New Jersey: Prentice-Hall, Inc., 1983.

An almost scientific approach, for the serious animal painter.

Van Gelder, Patricia. *Wildlife Artists at Work.* New York: Watson-Guptill Company, 1982.

It is interesting to see how various artists work and live. This book shows, quite graphically, that no one technique is correct—developing your *own* is most important.

Watson, Ernest W. *Ernest Watson's Course in Pencil Drawing.* New York: Van Nostrand Reinhold Company Inc., 1978.

This is really four books in one; Watson explored the basics of classical pencil drawing.

West, Keith. *How to Draw Plants.* New York: Watson-Guptill Company, 1983.

This book covers the field of botanical illustration with beautiful drawings and paintings.

Many books make no attempt at being how-to's but are full of wonderful drawings, paintings, and field sketches that should prove inspirational. A few of my favorites include the following.

Arnosky, Jim. *Secrets of a Wildlife Watcher*. New York: Lothrop, Lee and Shepard Books, 1983.

This book is a pleasure, with more of Arnosky's wonderful pencil sketches and valuable hints on getting close enough to your ''quarry'' to draw it too.

Brockie, Keith. *One Man's Island: A Naturalist's Year*. New York, Harper and Row, 1984.

Beautiful sketches, plus a rare insight into an ecosystem of a remote Scottish island.

Fox, William T. *At the Sea's Edge*. Englewood Cliffs, New Jersey: Prentice-Hall, Inc., 1983. Although I may never see the Atlantic, the field sketches and drawings by Clare Walker Leslie in this book made me feel as if I knew the area well.

Johnson, Cathy. *The Local Wilderness: Observing Neighborhood Nature Through an Artist's Eye*. New York: Prentice Hall Press, 1987.

My natural-history book covers keeping a field sketchbook as well as a number of other subjects; illustrations may provide inspiration for the serious artist.

Jood, Ton De, and Anthonie Stolk. *The Backyard Bestiary*. New York: Alfred A. Knopf, Inc., 1980.

Delightful watercolor illustrations in an unusual style by Kees De Kiefte make this book a must for anyone interested in nature on an intimate scale.

Kuhn, Bob. *Animal Art of Bob Kuhn*. Cincinnati: North Light Books, 1982.

Bob Kuhn has a lively, vital style; I learn just from looking at his sketches.

Leopold, Aldo. *A Sand County Almanac and Sketches Here and There*. New York: Oxford University Press, Inc. 1970.

Leopold's book is one of the classics in the field of ecological awareness. It is richly illustrated by Charles W. Schwartz's sensitive pencil drawings.

Leslie, Clare Walker. *A Naturalist's Sketchbook: Pages from the Seasons of a Year*. New York: Dodd, Mead and Company, Inc., 1987.

Leslie's daybook is a revelation on the uses of field drawings to illuminate daily life and the discoveries found in our own backyards.

Marsh, Janet. *Janet Marsh's Nature Diary*. New York: William Morrow and Company, 1979.

With exquisite pencil and wash drawings of an English valley ecosystem threatened by a proposed roadway, Marsh's book is an eloquent plea to save the valley and its denizens from ''progress.''

Schwartz, Charles W. *Wildlife Drawings*. Jefferson City, Missouri: The Missouri Department of Conservation, 1980.

This big book of wildlife drawings, many of which appear in my book, contains work done by Schwartz over many years with the department. It is a feast of pencil and pen-and-ink-on-scratchboard drawings.

Simon & Schuster. *Simon & Schuster's Guide to Trees*. New York: Simon & Schuster, 1977.

Stokes, Donald W. *A Guide to Bird Behavior*. Boston: Little, Brown and Company, 1969.

The illustrations in this book are by Stokes and J. Fenwick Lansdowne;

Lansdowne is one of the best bird artists around.

Stokes, Donald, and Lillian Stokes. *A Guide to Enjoying Wildflowers*. Boston: Little, Brown and Company, 1984.

All of the Stokes Nature Guide series have lovely illustrations; this one features Deborah Prince's delicate, accurate watercolors.

Tunnicliffe, C. F. *Sketches of Bird Life*. Commentary by Robert Gillmor. New York: Watson-Guptill Company, 1981.

Tunnicliffe studied birds all his life. This book is a compendium of some of his thousands of drawings, paintings, and field sketches, fascinating for anyone interested in drawing, painting, *or* birds.

Warner, Glen. *Glen Loates: A Brush With Life*. New York: Harry N. Abrams, Inc., 1984.

Loates' exquisite paintings are based firmly on his field sketches, on-the-spot research for a lifelong career in painting wildlife. This book contains both sketches and finished works.

Zwinger, Ann. *Beyond the Aspen Grove*. New York: Random House, 1970.

Zwinger's sensitive pencil drawings were among my first introductions to field sketching—in her case, much more finished studies than many of my own rough scribbles.

Zwinger, Ann, and Edwin Way Teale. *A Conscious Stillness*. New York: Harper and Row, 1982.

Zwinger is still spending her time exploring this beautiful country, pencil in hand. These are only two of the many books she has authored, co-authored, and illustrated. If anything, her drawings become even better than they were in her first, *Beyond the Aspen Grove*.

Index

Hamil, Jim, 35, 69, 114
Hammer, Keith, 52
Hicks, Laney, 44, 150–51
hills, 77–78
Hopkins, Frances Anne, 24
Hopper, Edward, 42

imaging, 22
inks, 12, 13. *See also* Pen-and-ink
    drawings
    applied with a brush, 27
    in watercolor, 48, 75
insects, 99

James, Frederic, 79
Jaques, Francis Lee, 153

Kautzky, Ted, 44
Kirlian photography, 51
Kuhn, Bob, 102

landscapes
    abstraction in, 90–92
    composition of, 81
    distance in, 85–87
    elements of, 80
    formats for, 81
    intimate, 87–90
    light and shadow in, 90
    man-made objects in, 87
    perspective in, 82–85
    value patterns in, 81, 82, 90
Landscape with Cattle, 1846
    (Bingham), 82
Leathers, Mary, 75
leaves, 57, 67–68
Leonardo da Vinci, 8, 27
Leonid, 85
Leslie, Clare Walker, 24, 55,
    85, 96, 153
lichens, 59
light, 30, 33, 68–69, 90, 119.
    See also Shadow; Value
line drawings, 34, 52. *See
    also* Pen-and-ink drawings;
    Pencil
Loates, Glen, 93, 102
Lussier, Ernest, 128

Machetanz, Fred, 102
McKeehan, J. L., 92
mammals, 97–99, 101–3
masking fluid, 47
middle ground, 70–71, 82
minerals. *See* Rocks and minerals
Missouri Conservationist, The,
    119
Monet, Claude, 82, 135, 136
mood, 32–33
Moore, Charles Herbert, 24
Moore, Henry, 126
Morrison, Gordon, 139
mosses, 59
mountains, 77–78
mushrooms, 59

Natural Bridge (Ward), 85, 90
nature drawing
    benefits of, 7, 8, 131, 138–39
    and conservation, 131, 136–38

as contemplation, 131–33
and observation, 7–8, 21–22,
    50, 139–41, 153
planning, 21–22
special places for, 133–42
negative space, 33
Nympheas (Monet), 82

observation, 7–8, 21–22, 139–41
    and animal drawing, 93–94, 96,
        153
    and geological drawing, 77
    and plant drawing, 50–51, 53–54
oil painting, 128
O'Keeffe, Georgia, 92, 135
Olive Grove, The, (van Gogh), 82

paints, 13–14, 38. *See also*
    Watercolor
palettes, 18, 36–38
paper
    bond, 14, 19
    cold-press, 14
    colored, 14
    hot-press, 14
    for pencil drawing, 25
    pH of, 14
    rough, 14
    stretching, 38–39
    textures of, 14
    watercolor, 14, 38–39, 49
pastels, 148–49, 151
pen-and-ink drawings, 11–13, 26–28,
    74, 144–46. *See also*
    Inks; Pens
pencil, 9–11, 20, 24–26, 73–74
    charcoal, 11
    colored, 11, 148, 151
    hardness of, 9, 24, 25
    and line weight, 24
    mechanical, 9–11, 20
    paper for, 25
    shading with, 24, 25
    sharpening, 11
    soft, 25–26
pens. *See also* Inks; Pen-and-ink
    drawings
    ball-point, 12–13, 20
    bamboo, 12
    calligraphy, 26
    felt-tipped, 20
    nibs for, 11–12
    sketch, 12, 26
    technical, 12, 26
perspective, 52, 82–85
Peterson, Roger Tory, 34, 99
pets, 97–99
phantom drawing, 23
photography
    advantages of drawing over,
        80–81
    color in, 112, 114
    and composition, 112, 114
    copying of, 118
    and copyright, 117
    equipment for, 113–14
    and format, 114
    Kirlian, 51
    for research, 112, 114–17,
        117–18, 144, 150, 151

as sketch substitutes, 114–17
    use of others', 117–18
Picasso, Pablo, 126
Pike, John, 13, 18, 71
planning, 9, 21–22, 81, 106
plants. *See also* Trees
    field sketches of, 51
    flowers, 54–55, 59–60
    foreshortening of, 52
    leaves, 57
    lichens, 59
    minuscule, 60–61
    mosses, 59
    mushrooms, 59
    observation of, 50–51, 53–54
    seasonal, 57–58
    specimens of, 52–53
    value patterns of, 52
Port Jefferson (Leonid), 85
Potter, Beatrix, 153
pottery, 128
printmaking, 128

rainbows, 34–35, 49
Rathbun, Carolyn Dorsey, 151
Reid, Charles, 23, 88
Rembrandt, 27, 42, 79, 135
rocks and minerals
    origins of, 72
    pen-and-ink drawings of, 74–75
    pencil drawings of, 73–74
    study of, 77
    textures of, 73–75
    watercolor paintings of, 75
Rubens, Peter Paul, 27, 79

Salo, Bob, 128
salt, 46–47, 75
Saral paper, 125
Schwartz, Charles W., 27, 114,
    119, 144
scientific illustration, 9, 27,
    34, 60, 67, 119, 123, 146–47,
    151
scratchboard, 14–16, 74–75
scumbling, 68
Seton, Ernest Thompson, 153
shadow, 30–31, 34. *See also*
    Light; Value
    in landscapes, 90
    and trees, 64–65, 69, 71
shrubs, 65. *See also* Trees
*Simon & Schuster's Guide to
    Trees,* 34
sketchbooks
    as diaries, 105–7
    as field journals, 20, 105–11
    landscape sketches in, 81
    notes in, 109–11
    as planning space, 106
    as record, 108–9
    tree sketches in, 62, 66–67
    value sketches in, 32, 81
Sorenson, Carol, 147–48
spatter, 13, 46
sponging, 49, 68
Stegner, Charles, 128
Stewart, John, 133, 151
stippling, 27, 75
Stolzenberger, Sharon, 146

Other Books from Design Press

CALLIGRAPHY TIPS by Bill Gray

Even the most experienced calligrapher will appreciate a helping hand from Bill Gray, professional artist, graphic designer, teacher, and best-selling author. Gray's latest book of tips explores the various styles of lettering, major written alphabets, basic tools, materials, and techniques. Covering the design and execution of one-of-a-kind cards, invitations, and certificates, it also includes hints on style, ways to improve speed and quality, safety precautions, sources of supply, organizations to contact, advice on selling calligraphy, and, above all, Bill Gray's unique solutions to the problems routinely encountered by anyone pursuing lettering, either as a hobby or as a career. '' . . . Gray's books provide calligraphers and graphic artists [with] an excellent encyclopedia of practical information and techniques . . . When you come up with a graphic arts problem, you think you have to solve alone, if you consult Bill Gray's Books of Tips, you'll probably find the help you are looking for,'' says *Scripsit*, a publication of the Washington Calligraphers Guild.

Paperback $12.95   Book No. 50001

THE VISUAL NATURE OF COLOR by Patricia Sloane

What is color? Is our perception of color limited by the words we use to describe it? What is the relationship between color and light? Between color and form? How have our cultural preconceptions about color affected our theorizing about it? What should students be taught about color theory? Are there primary colors? Are color harmony and complementarity meaningful concepts? This text considers these and many other questions, incorporating and analyzing theories from the sciences, philosophy, and the arts. Rethinking old ideas while considering new ones, Patricia Sloane encourages a fresh perspective on the phenomenology of color, helping the reader to think in visual terms, to reason about visual phenomena; applying an artist's point of view to draw theory into a general philosophy of design. An important and scholarly study, THE VISUAL NATURE OF COLOR will interest students and instructors of art and art history, artists and designers, and those concerned with color in other fields, such as psychology and industry.

Hardcover $27.95   Book No. 50000

*Prices subject to change without notice

Look for Design Press books at your local bookstore or write

Design Press
P.O. Box 40
Blue Ridge Summit, PA
17294-0580

TO ORDER TOLL-FREE: 1-800-233-1128